THE
EXPLODING
CITY

THE EXPLODING CITY

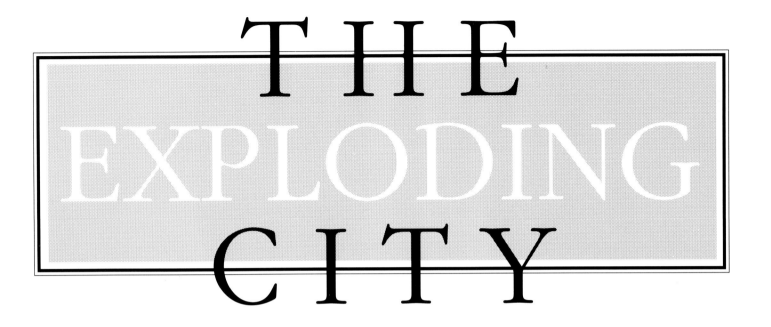

TEXT BY ROBERT L. SCHIFFER
PHOTOGRAPHS BY JERRY COOKE

FOREWORD BY ISAAC ASIMOV

ST. MARTIN'S PRESS
NEW YORK

Design by Robert Bull Design

Library of Congress Cataloging-in-Publication Data

Schiffer, Robert L.
The exploding city / Robert L. Schiffer; photographs by Jerry Cooke.
p.   cm.
ISBN 0-312-02361-8
1. Cities and towns.   2. Metropolitan areas.   3. City and town
life.   I. Title.
HT151.S276   1989   88-11596
307.7′64—dc19

First Edition

10 9 8 7 6 5 4 3 2 1

CONTENTS

This book has been made possible by the United Nations Population Fund and its late Executive Director, Rafael M. Salas, a farsighted and compassionate man who helped give new meaning to the word "population." To him, to his successor, Dr. Nafis Sadik, and to all his colleagues who had the vision to foresee the implications a new urban world had for an already dangerously overcrowded and congested planet, this book is gratefully dedicated.

ACKNOWLEDGMENTS

No acknowledgments can properly convey the huge debt we owe to the many who so generously helped us in the preparation of this book. This is especially true of the mayors, other city officials, urban experts, and everyone else who extended both hospitality and assistance in the nine cities we visited. And, incidentally, given the realities and inevitable toll of urban politics (a universal condition), if some of the mayors pictured in the city profiles are no longer in office when this book appears, we still want them to know how appreciative we are. All told, the list of everyone we should thank is much too long to include here, and this is a dilemma with particular relevance to all the gifted men and women of the United Nations Population Fund we had the privilege of meeting both at its headquarters in New York and in its field offices around the world. Much of this book reflects the knowledge and perspectives they unstintingly shared with us. But a special word of appreciation is due to Jyoti Singh and Edmund Kerner for their invaluable advice and encouragement, and to Sethuramiah S. N. Rao and Hirofumi Ando for their keen insights and many wise suggestions. Our thanks also to Stephen Viederman and Alex Marshall for their help and cooperation, and to Lois Jones, who always knew how to make the unworkable work. A. S. Karlikow and Walter Mertens were most valued and helpful critics; Norman Ho's unrelenting eye probed the text; Elizabeth Pope and Image Photo Laboratory developed and printed the pictures with a rare blend of care and craft; and Lolita Sia somehow deciphered the notes and manuscript more than once. We are grateful to all of them, as we are to George Witte, our editor at St. Martin's Press, for his imagination, good humor, and endurance.

And perhaps the last should be first, this book is for Barbara and Selma.

R.L.S. and J.C.

FOREWORD

THE BIRTH OF THE CITY

by Isaac Asimov

Homo sapiens (or, as we sometimes refer to ourselves, "modern man") is at least 50,000 years old. For four-fifths of that time, human beings lived the lives of hunters and gatherers, wandering over their territory in search of food. They were never able to linger long in one locality, for they would soon strip it of its most readily available food supply and they would then have to move on.

What changed matters was the development of herding and agriculture some 10,000 years ago. People learned to gather animals together, to take care of them, and to foster their reproduction. They could make use of their wool, their milk, their eggs, their capacity to do undemanding work. They could even cull out their numbers and eat some.

Even more important was the taming of edible plants, fostering their growth, removing weeds, driving off animals competing for the food, harvesting the plants at last, preparing it for food while saving the seed for replanting at an appropriate time.

Life grew harder as a result. Caring for animals was a demanding task. Caring for plants was even worse, demanding months of back-breaking work that might come to nothing if there was a failure of the rains, or a hailstorm, or a plague of insects.

Undoubtedly, there remained a memory (growing dimmer with time) of an earlier kind of life in which food was simply gathered. Legends of a "golden age" proliferated, and the best one known to us is that of the Garden of Eden, from which Adam and Eve were expelled, and compelled to get their food, as farmers, by "the sweat of their brow."

And yet there was no return to the "simpler" life. The fact was that herding and agriculture vastly increased the food supply and, therefore, the population of those engaging in these activities. To abandon herding and agriculture, after it had become well-established, meant mass-starvation. The tiger was firmly held by its tail.

Herding still involved a wandering life, for if human beings had their food supply more secure in the form of their animals, those animals had to be led to pasture, and had to be transferred from place to place in an unending search for more grazing.

Agriculture (which produced more food per acre and, therefore, a higher density of population, than herding did) introduced something entirely new, however. Farms could not move and farmers were nailed to the ground, so to speak. For the first time, sizable groups of human beings came into existence who were essentially immobile.

The growing supply of food on the farms was bound to encourage the acquisitive instincts of surrounding non-farmers of one sort or another, who would have no objection to collecting the food they had not worked for. If they appeared, the farmers simply could not decide that discretion was the better part of valor, and run off. If they did, their food supply vanished and they would starve. They had no choice but to stand and fight.

Being human beings, they did their best to increase their chances by gathering together and building their houses in a group so that they could fight together, with less chance of being isolated and defeated in detail. They established their houses on a hill with a secure water supply, stocked it with a food supply, and built a wall around it, so they could sally forth to fight, and retreat back into it at choice (or at need) as a sure refuge.

In short, agriculture meant the development of what we now call cities, though the first ones were tiny representatives of the species with a population of no more than a few hundred.

With time, of course, the cities grew and so did the extent of the farms surrounding the city, and the whole became what we now call a "city-state."

The growing farms meant a surplus of food in good years, so that some of the city dwellers had food available for themselves that they didn't have to grow. Of course, they had to give something in exchange—pottery, baskets, or other artifacts that they could make and farmers could use. Or else they paid for the food in services; some were skilled at fighting, some at governing, some at priestcraft.

In short, the cities fostered specialization, and complexity of organizations. Our word "citizen" means "city dweller" and our word "civilization" comes from the Latin word for a "city dweller." In short, agriculture begat cities, which begat civilization.

The first city-states grew up about rivers—the Euphrates, the Nile, the Indus, the Hwang-Ho—since these supplied a reliable source of water needed for agriculture. To make full use of the water, there had to be the digging of canals to lead water to the farming areas, dykes to prevent flooding, dredging to keep water-level low, and so on.

This worked best if the various city-states along the course of a river cooperated with each other. Such cooperation was most easily assured if one of the city-states dominated the others, made decisions for all of them, and was in a position to enforce those decisions. In this way, the first nations and empires were built up.

In short, the consequences of cities had both their admirable and their less admirable aspects. If cities meant the growth of artisanry and technology, they also meant the growth of war and oppression.

Cities, which first came into being about 8000 B.C., remained relatively small for thousands of years. It was only in the final quarter of their existence that big cities arose: Memphis, Thebes, Babylon, Athens, Rome, Alexandria, to say nothing of a number in India and China.

And even so, the big cities remained few in number and the world in general consisted of rural areas and villages—even as late as the opening of the twentieth century. It was only in our century and particularly after World War II that there came to be an urban explosion, with results that are described in this book, *The Exploding City.*

Robert Schiffer and Jerry Cooke explain the present situation in detail in a timely, thought-provoking account of a situation that, without question, is one of the overriding issues of our age. In the course of my own lifetime, the earth's population has increased two and a half times, and most of this increase is now to be found in the exploding urban centers, especially in the slums and shantytowns, of Africa, Asia, and Latin America. And before another century is out, as they tell us, there will be more people packed into these same cities than everyone put together on the entire planet today.

Schiffer and Cooke literally take us on an eye-opening journey for an intimate, behind-the-scenes look at this emerging new world of the city, and I can only hope the book will be widely read and taken to heart. For this is no imaginary world of the future that they picture, but a real world already here, one in which the city, overfilled and troubled, has become the symbol of our common hopes and humanity. We are not prepared for this world, but unless we act now before it is too late, the city, which originated civilization, may in the end destroy it.

INTRODUCTION

—tomorrow is our permanent address . . .

—e.e. cummings

The Exploding City is about the new urban world now being born. It is about cities desperately racing to catch up with a tomorrow already made obsolete by the reality of today. We have, for the most part, been taken by surprise, and that in itself is no small paradox considering that we hardly needed any time at all to learn the secret of nuclear fission, or how to build a spaceship, or compress everything we know and more onto a microchip. The city has been with us for thousands of years, and we are just beginning to realize how little we know about it.

The problems all cities face—New York no less than Mexico City, Tokyo no less than Cairo, Rome no less than Bombay—only point up how poorly prepared we are to enter this new age of the city. The danger is that while we feel our way, the city is becoming the catalyst for radical changes in the world's social, economic, and political life. In short, there can no longer be a distinction between the welfare of the city and the welfare of the nation—and of the entire fragile planet itself. They are inseparable.

For all that, however, the unchecked, unplanned growth of cities, particularly in the poorer developing countries of the Third World, is not the exception but the rule in these closing years of a century that opened with not the faintest hint of the explosion to come. In 1900, less than 10 percent of the world's population lived in urban communities, and even as late as 1920, the total was less than 14 percent. After that, the change was sudden and decisive, climbing to more than 40 percent by the mid-1980s. By the year 2000, it will top 50 percent and keep going. The statistics are mind-boggling:

- 400,000 in 1900, 1 million in 1940, 18 million in 1986, 26 million in 2000.

- 1 million in 1930, 3.5 million in 1950, 10 million in 1986, 16 million in 2000.
- 3 million in 1950, 6 million in 1970, 9 million in 1986, 16 million in 2000.

Mexico City—Cairo—Bombay. Three widely separated Third World cities. Three almost identical explosions. And the same is true for São Paulo, Djakarta, Kinshasa, Lagos, Calcutta—and a dozen or two more cities, all huge, massive, sprawling agglomerations leading the way into the new urban world of the next century.

But explosive statistics, for all their shock value, are not the full story. For that one must look behind the bare numbers, and that is the intent of this book. In the course of our research, we went to nine cities, some of them exploding, some of them not, but each a key link in what Rafael Salas called "an emerging worldwide urban conglomerate."

The cities, in the order visited, were Mexico City, New York, Tokyo, Shanghai, Bombay, Moscow, Rome, Cairo, and Lagos. We chose them because they make up a global cross-section geographically, economically, and politically, and because together they offer a glimpse of what much of the world will look like in the year 2000. As will be pointed out in the pages that follow, each city, rich or poor, has its own special problems and its own priorities in dealing with them. And these priorities, in turn, are colored by its own mix of history, its own life-style and culture. Together, however, cities share a community of concerns—some of the problems are startling in their sameness—and their joint urban experiences cut through international, ideological, and cultural differences. Indeed, if there is a common denominator in the world today—an experience that people all over share and that in a sense unites them—it is to be found in the unique interrelationship that exists between a city and its people caught up together in a historic and dramatic transition that has still to run its course.

The pictures taken in the nine cities we visited try to show how this transition is touching the lives of the people involved at various stages of the human life cycle. The text tries to put what is happening to them into perspective, providing general background on the explosion and, we hope, answering a few questions about it.

The United Nations Population Fund has held two international conferences dealing with the urban explosion and its direct ties with a global population that has already broken the five-billion mark and is well on its way to six. The first conference was in Rome in 1980, and the second in Barcelona in 1986, both of them bringing together mayors whose giant cities are at the heart of it all. We have drawn liberally from their discussions and from the documentation that grew out of these conferences, and we are indebted to the Fund for making them available for our use.

Finally, *The Exploding City* is not intended as a guidebook for the tourist, nor as a source book for the expert, although we hope it will appeal to both. But above all, our larger aim is that it will be a book for anyone interested in one of the great human dramas of today.

Robert L. Schiffer
Jerry Cooke

THE
EXPLODING
CITY

ONE

My room is like a
closed up well.
Outside there is smog,
Where shall my mind roam.

—Balswarup Rahi

By the year 2000, for the first time in history, more than half the people on earth will live in cities now exploding across the globe on a scale and with a speed never before dreamed possible. Barring the unpredictable or unthinkable, a new urban world will come into being when the new millennium dawns.

Until very recently, most of us were not even aware any such event was impending, much less of its magnitude in an era that has already seen mankind crack the atom and blast off into space. But it is inevitable that the birth of an urban world should affect most, if not all, of humanity; so its genesis may well go down as one of the milestones of the century just drawing to a close.

Whatever the ultimate judgment of history, the evidence has been building since mid-century, as has the momentum. By the time Mexico City's population soared above 18 million and it became the largest city in the world in 1986, there was no turning back. Ironically, Mexico City was then still counting the dead left by a devastating earthquake it had suffered some months earlier, an accident of timing that only served to symbolize how inevitable the urban future is and how little can stop it.

When that future arrives, Mexico City, for all its vast size, will not be unique. Rather, it will be—as it already is—the very epitome of the exploding city, one of a new breed of metropolises unmatched in human experience that now literally are changing the face of our planet. We have yet to come up with a name for this revolutionary

3

phenomenon, but we see it reaching out, creating bloated, congested cities, few of them really prepared for the human tide engulfing them.

Much the greater part of this sudden explosion is centered in a Third World that in the twenty-first century will still be poor, if not poorer, than it is now; still the scene of an ongoing mass migration, perhaps the greatest in history, that is pouring out of the countryside and into the cities; and still the home of most of the world's population, which, in the few remaining years of the twentieth century, will jump from the already record-high five billion that it hit in mid-1987 to more than six billion in the year 2000.

Only little more than a generation ago, the shift from city to *megalopolis* (the term that caught on in the 1960s) marked a leap of one order of magnitude as cities in the West and the rest of the industrialized world in particular sprawled beyond their accustomed limits to gobble up the green space between them and form new-style urban agglomerations, the size of which had not been equaled before then. Now an almost exponential increase has become the mark of the giant city of the Third World, where even the boundaries of *megalopolis* have burst and a new *hypercity* (for lack of something better to call it) is taking shape.

This awesome progression is only one aspect of a still wider upheaval in the Third World, in which smaller cities, too, as well as towns and villages of all sizes—old and new alike—are multiplying and swelling to unexpected, unheard-of dimensions to make room for the new and growing urban majority. And the end is not in sight.

Clearly, even as we need a new name for this phenomenon, so, too, we require some broader frame of reference to understand what is happening—and what promises to happen—because of it. For in these final years of the twentieth century it has become evident that urban problems, long on the back burner of global issues, are not only emerging to take their place among the most urgent of our day, but that soon they may overshadow most others.

There are those who maintain that the future of the city may well determine the future of the world. But whether it does or it does not, it is already evident that when we enter the new urban world in the next few years, we will find ourselves in largely unexplored territory, knowing more about the distant planets of outer space than about the exploding cities of our own planet Earth. While we feel our way, momentous changes wll be taking place, generated by a fallout we are just beginning to recognize for what it really is.

TWO

The overcrowding, the congestion, the housing shortages, the slums and shantytowns, the homeless, the rural refugees, the pollution, the traffic jams—signs of the explosion have been with us for a long time, common sights in much of the world. We have grown so accustomed to seeing them—they have etched their way so deeply into our consciousness—that we now take it for granted they are a normal part of the same old, familiar landscape of the city, as always, in transition.

Even as the voyager in space-time is not truly aware of how he is affected by it, so, we, in the midst of all this urban upheaval, hardly can be faulted if we have been slow in sensing the true nature of what has been taking place all around us. Someone born in, say 1920, came into a world where 86 percent of its then two billion or so people still were attached to the land, or to the small town that served the needs of the rural population around it. This attachment shaped attitudes and ways of thought, as well as the rhythms of toil and celebration fashioned *mores,* as well as routines. It helped decide individual personal goals as well as setting parameters of larger public policy for the great majority.

Today world population has soared spectacularly to five billion and more, and the proportion of those who no longer have this direct attachment to earth and agriculture, with its own environment and quality of air and water, has risen to well over 40 percent. The bulk of this increase has come about since 1950, with the number of people living in cities tripling in the next thirty-five years. For better or worse, the spectrum, the vision, and the environment of these two billion people—as many as existed in all the world in 1920—is urban, with consequences for the ways in which people now think and relate to each other. Very soon, when their number rises to 50 percent, and higher still, their urban destiny will be the destiny of most of the world.

For all practical purposes, today's communications and transportation have made distance and natural barriers such as mountains, oceans, and deserts all but meaningless. So while the developing countries of Africa, Asia, and Latin America are at the epicenter of the explosion, the fallout is global, and reverberations are already being felt on a broad spectrum of the world's economic, social, and political life. We are thus affected by the explosion no matter where we live, in an exploding city or not. The sooner, therefore, we fully understand what *is* happening and plan for what *will* happen, the easier and safer will be the earth's metamorphosis into what is already being called a *planetopolis*.

The notion of a huge space city floating in its own lonely corner of the galaxy is not some weird science-fiction concept of a futuristic world, but rather the product of serious demographic studies that see today's widely disparate and scattered cities emerging as "tomorrow's neighborhoods," linking key points on an urban earth. Indeed, if we use "urban" just to describe populated centers of 20,000 and more, the sheer number now coming into existence is staggering.

What is most astounding about this transition is both its speed and its suddenness. Mankind has been living in organized settlements for at least fifteen thousand to twenty thousand years, but the city itself as we know it probably did not evolve until about the fourth millennium before Christ. Although it marked the beginning of a new phase of human history—from the outset the city was both a symbol of power and the center of economic, political, and intellectual life—urban living was to remain relatively limited until the 1800s. Before then, fewer than ten people in one thousand on the globe lived in a town or city.

Beginning with Ur, it was not size that singled out storied cities of history—King David's Jerusalem, the Rome of the Caesar's, Timbuktu at its height, medieval Paris, and more—all cities great in their time. Changan (present-day Xian), the imperial capital of the Tang dynasty, reached one million in the ninth century, but it was anomoly of an elevated status not to be achieved again, except in China, until London, sparked by the industrial revolution, also attained that eminence in the nineteenth century.

But even then it took London 130 years to grow from one million to eight. Consider, in contrast, how long it took Mexico City. A peaceful, bucolic 400,000 in 1900, Mexico City hit the one-million mark in 1940. Barely thirty years later, by 1970, it had multiplied itself by eight, and then more than doubled that in the next sixteen years, to top 18 million by the end of 1986. Come the year 2000, Mexico City will have some 26 million people according to official government estimates (although some demographers think it may well be more).

The story is much the same in Cairo, now 10 million strong, or ten times what it was in 1930, and expected to reach at least 16 million by the year 2000. It repeats itself in Bombay, where a congested population of 9 million, triple what it was in 1950, is well on the way to 16 million and more before the end of the century. In São Paulo, in Djakarta, in Kinshasa, in Lagos, in Calcutta—in virtually every Third World city—statistics once thought spectacular, if not unbelievable, are now routine. Choked by a relentless growth, the older cities spill past long-established boundaries, and brand-new ones spring up, as if by magic, almost overnight. Some are dusty villages one day; bewildered, ill-prepared giant metropolises the next. Others are built from scratch in jungles and deserts that were once impenetrable or uninhabitable, but are now ringed, crisscrossed, and pock marked with roads, rails, and airports.

No longer is the *mega-city,* the *megalopolis,* the *hypercity* a curiosity or a rarity. In 1950, there were only ten agglomerations of 5 million and more inhabitants, six of them in the more developed countries: New York, London, Tokyo, Paris, Chicago, and Rhein-Ruhr (which is really not a city but a metropolitan conglomeration of several cities). By the end of the century, these one-time urban aristocrats will have become all but commonplace: the U.N. projects that there will be at least 48 of them, and that 37 will be in the less-developed countries.

The shift taking place in the world's urban balance is seen even more starkly if one looks at the list of what is shaping up to be the top 25 cities in the year 2000, the smallest of them just under 10 million. Only six will be in the industrialized world—Tokyo, New York, Los Angeles, London, Osaka, and Moscow—and all the rest, 19 (including the top two, Mexico City and São Paulo), will be in the Third World, with many more looming on the horizon. By 2025, the number of these urban giants is expected to exceed 90, with some 80 of them in the poorer countries.

The rate of expansion at lower levels is equally astounding. Urban centers of a hundred thousand and more are replacing traditional towns and villages, and the city of at least a million, once something special, is sprouting everywhere. After an increase of only nine—from two to eleven—in the entire nineteenth century, the number of urban "millionaires," as they have been called, shot up to seventy-five in the first half of the twentieth century, most of them in the industrialized world. But then, in the next thirty years, the total multiplied itself several times over to reach 222 by 1980, more than half in developing countries. And by the year 2025, that total is expected to triple.

Here we see another major trend of our times. Again using 1920 as the jumping-off point, only the industrialized countries of Europe (where massive urbanization started after the industrial revolution; less than three percent of the world's population was urban at the time) were then approaching their urban majority, which they attained in 1950 together with Japan. Africa, Asia, and Latin America (with

certain exceptions) were still largely rural and remained so until
World War II. Then the change began, slowly at first but building up
speed much like a gathering avalanche. And in little more than a
generation, the developing world, looked at as a whole, had attained
its urban majority, too, doing in a few years what it had taken the rest
of the world all of history to accomplish. For the better part of this
century, London, New York, and Tokyo—in that order—had taken

THE 25 LARGEST CITIES IN THE YEAR 2000

Mexico City	25.8 million
São Paulo	24.0
Tokyo	20.2
Calcutta	16.5
Bombay	16.0
New York	15.8
Seoul	13.8
Teheran	13.6
Shanghai	13.3
Rio de Janeiro	13.3
Buenos Aires	13.2
Djakarta	13.2
Delhi	13.2
Karachi	12.0
Dacca	11.2
Manila	11.1
Cairo	11.1
Los Angeles	11.0
Bangkok	10.7
London	10.5
Osaka	10.5
Moscow	10.4
Beijing	10.4
Lima	9.1
Tianjin	9.1

SOURCE: The United Nations Population Fund

turns as the largest city in the world. When Mexico City shot to the top in 1986, it became the first city in a developing country to assume what is now a questionable distinction at best.

Today Latin America is 70 percent urbanized, Africa and Asia 30 percent, statistics that jump upward even as they are compiled—Africa's fastest and highest of all (it will surpass North America by the turn of the century). All together, by the year 2000, the developing countries will have a combined city population of 2 billion people, nearly seven times what they had in 1950 and just about double the urban population of the entire industrialized world. And then a quarter of a century later—by 2025—with a projected 3.9 billion people, it will be quadruple, with more to come. At this rate, fears are mounting that the urban environment of the new world now taking shape could well become unliveable.

There has been nothing like it ever before. The logistics and cost of providing liveable conditions for so many people in such a short space of time are staggering—even if it could be done and even if the money needed to do it could be found. To keep up with today's rate, according to the World Commission on Environment and Development, by the end of the century the Third World would have to increase by 65 percent the capacity it now has to produce and manage its urban infrastructure, services, and shelter. And even if by some miracle it did so (and that means coming up with housing, utilities, schools, hospitals, commercial structure, transportation, and everything else the equivalent of some 1600 functioning new "millionaire" cities would need), it would still only be enough to maintain present conditions. It would not take care of the billion already homeless, and the slums, the shantytowns, the congestion, the deplorable conditions under which most of the Third World lives would still be with us.

As Robert S. McNamara, the former president of the World Bank has put it, the huge urban agglomerations of the West took a long time to build up their housing stocks, physical infrastructures, and public amenities. The giant cities of the Third World, however, will have doubled themselves and more in just half a century, and their sizes already are such that any economies of location are dwarfed by costs of their congestion.

"The rapid population growth that has produced them," he says, "has far outpaced the growth of human and physical infrastructure needed for even moderately efficient economic life and orderly political and social relationships, let alone amenities for their residents. . . ."

In short, the experiences of Europe and the rest of the industrialized world are not all that much help to Third World cities that today are up against a situation far more critical and demanding than any city anywhere, or at any time, has ever faced.

THREE

But the impoverished cities of the Third World are not the only ones in trouble. Many of the wealthier cities of Europe and North America—and Japan, too—in a sense now on the sidelines of the explosion, have serious problems of their own. As they are discovering urbanization is not always a process of growth alone; it is also a constant process of renewal. They have the resources the poorer cities lack, but they are in trouble because their infrastructures—built up over generations—sorely need updating, and the cost of keeping them in repair has now become acute. Urban ghettos have become commonplace in all too many of them, and a changing technology and competition have weakened the industrial base on which these cities built their wealth.

With poverty as one of its most serious problems today, New York City provides a dramatic example of what is happening in more than one pace-setting Western city. Indeed, several are recasting priorities and approaches, in one case to offset the rusting of what had been a powerful manufacturing center, in another to make up for the flight from a once-vigorous inner city area to the surrounding suburbs that left it with a much diminished tax base for needed services.

In some of the most urbanized areas of North America and Europe, the population dominance of the majority of cities has decreased in places like France and West Germany, and cities in Japan, too, are feeling the pinch. Meanwhile, cities like Detroit and Paris, even New York, have at least temporarily declined not only in relative, but in absolute terms as well; and, overall, the years leading up to the year 2000 are seen as a time of intense economic reappraisal and readjustment. This is especially true for cities in the industrial world in which the number of people over the age of sixty and sixty-five is steadily rising, as is the case in the United States, Europe, and Japan.

The United States Bureau of the Census points out that one of the most significant demographic facts affecting the world is the aging of its population, which has been occurring because of a decline in previously high fertility rates and increases in life expectancy since 1950. There are now 286 million people in the world sixty-five years of age or older, and this figure will increase to 418 million by the year 2000. In the United States, for example, the over-sixty-five percentage will increase from 12 percent in 1985 to 19.5 percent in 2025; in Japan, where the elderly proportion is increasing faster than in any other country, it will double from 10 percent to 20.3 percent.

This transformation of society will be most noticeable in the big cities. In New York City, nearly one in every five persons is past the age of sixty. Rome and Tokyo are not far behind, and Moscow, among others, is right up there, too, as a growing number of "pensioners" become an ever more important part of the city's population.

The situation in Third World cities is quite the reverse. They will mark the year 2000 still relatively youthful. But there will be some exceptions, notably in China, where its so-called baby boom generation will start turning into the aging generation in the first quarter of the new century. By 2025, the proportion of China's elderly will more than double, a development particularly evident in Shanghai, where the city is beginning to worry about where it will find the labor force it needs for its ports and industries in the new century.

In one way or another, cities all over the world are entering a new era and coping with new sets of circumstances to which they must adjust almost overnight. Over the millenia before this, since cities first sprang up—whether originally as a settlement for protection, military advantage, or a geographic and trading crossroads—changes in their development were a slow-evolving process. For example, well-developed patterns of construction emerged over a period of time. An inhabitant, say, of Jericho, one of the world's oldest known urban settlements, believed to have been founded some 8000 years ago, would have found familiar elements in the outlay and spatial use of cities built hundreds and even thousands of years later right through the centuries prior to the central location of religious and government institutions and markets.

Within the city, in these same centuries, there would be radical transformation of economic activity, through specialization and concentration. Urban life would create its own, new sets of social relationships—persons being bound by crafts and guilds, say, rather than by land tenure—and one new urban class after another eventually would come into being: most lately the bourgeoisie, setting fashion in style and culture as well as government; and the working proletariat, as much forged by the factories that sucked them in as any of the products they produced.

Urban architecture and arteries, and the growth of special town quarters, would reflect all these changes, in guild hall and mansion, factory, tenement, and slum. For all that, and for all the city's dominance in the progress of civilization, as recently as 1800, less than one person in a hundred on the globe dwelt in a town or city, yet the urban concentration became "the most efficient mechanism for accomplishing complex, gigantic, and productive tasks." The city, in short, has proven to be a remarkably flexible and resilient instrument for social absorption, innovation, and change.

But can cities of the Third World still do that today, given the sudden pace of their growth this past century and the even more feverish acceleration of recent decades? What must be considered in any response is whether the city is still a dynamo of social and economic development as it was in past years or whether it has developed to the point where it now stands in the way of healthy growth. Is it, as Harvard population scientist Walter Mertens has asked, a burden or a blessing? The answers are mixed.

For all who argue that the city has been, and remains, the heart and soul of industry, a stimulus to mass education and greater literacy, a home for the great libraries and museums and the theaters that enrich culture, a promoter of science and technology, there are those who believe that the human costs simply are too much, too high in terms of pollution, environmental degradation, increased delinquency, crime, and personal and family disorganization and disintegration; that cities no longer can effectively fulfill fundamental demands for shelter and employment for great numbers; that already, in many of the world's great cities, as many as 30 to 60 percent and more of the population live in slums or squatter colonies whose names (*paracaiastas,* or parachute jumpers, in Mexico; *gecekondu,* night flyers, in Turkey) are as colorful as the barrios and ghettos themselves are dismal and poverty-rampant.

No matter whether one is optimist or pessimist, however, the causes that make for the current urban explosion now lie beyond the power of any one country to alter. In most of the world, people are voting with their feet, and migrating from countryside to town and city.

FOUR

How to explain this rush to the city? What is it that drives the Egyptian *fellah* from the lands his ancestors have tilled since the days of the *Pharaohs*? What is it that unites him with the Mexican *campesino* he has never seen, nor likely ever will? What is it that sparked almost simultaneous explosions in Egypt and in Mexico, in Nigeria, in India, in Brazil—in countries oceans and continents apart—and started what is now perhaps the biggest and most massive human migration in history?

Not one, but two fuses set it off: poverty and population. To take the second first, the urbanization of the planet is the inevitable next step for a world now on the way to tripling itself in this century alone. It took from the beginning of time until about 1830 for global population to reach its first billion, and then one hundred years more to double that by 1930. The next three billion combined took less than sixty years and, one spring day in mid-1987, the earth was a planet of five billion people!

As remarkable as the speed of this growth has been its steadiness. The expectation is that by the year 2000 the total world population will exceed six billion, by 2010 seven, by 2022 eight, and still going strong—although many demographers believe the global growth rate will have reached its peak by then and begin to level off, stabilizing at about 10 billion at the end of the twenty-first century. For now, however, the world is growing at an estimated one million people every four to five days, with 90 percent of this increase in a Third World where nine of ten babies are already being born to a population still largely made up of young people not yet in their child-bearing prime. In Africa, for example, for every 100 people, 55 of them are under 20.

In most countries of Europe, in the United States, Japan, and in a few other countries in the wealthier industrialized world, the growth rate is down to less than one percent; in the poorer developing countries, it is still over two percent. The picture is uneven from region to region, but even where fertility rates have dropped sharply, the overall population growth rate is up—in rural areas no less than in the cities—as improved health conditions bring longer life and lower death rates. Or seen from another perspective, overall population is going up not just because there are more births, but because there are more survivors!

To look at Africa again, the United Nations Population Fund foresees a birth rate there in 2025 that will be down to 25 per 1000, a cut of almost half. But by then the number of women who will reach child-bearing age will be up to 430 million; so even with a lowered birthrate, there still will be 42 million more births that year.

Today, looking at the developing world as a whole, the Population Reference Bureau in Washington, D.C., cautions that with its population growing at 2.1 percent annually, there is good reason to dispute "a popular notion" that the era of rapid population growth is over. So fast has it been, in fact, that for all the millions now flocking to cities, there are millions more being born in a desperately poor countryside, and here we come to the first of the two fuses setting off the urban explosion. The grinding poverty that is now endemic to the rural areas of the developing countries. The land can no longer support its people or feed them; and in those places where it does produce, it is being taken over by big farming combines. Added to that, untold acreage, as in the African famine belt, has been overused and abused to such an extent that it can no longer grow crops, not even with rainfall. The number of "environmental refugees" who thus take to the roads is hard to estimate, but during the first half of the 1980s at least 10 million Africans were forced off the land; most those who did not die of disease or starvation wound up in urban squatter settlements or refugee camps.

While not the victims of famine, the *fellah* and the *campesino,* and millions of their counterparts in other Third World countries, are also fleeing a land so dismally unproductive they cannot scratch a living out of the barren soil. Nor can they find work in a rural area that is economically stagnant and shows little prospect of getting better. For all of them, therefore, the only alternative is to leave and head to the cities where the jobs are, a desperate flight to save themselves, with no guarantees at the end of it.

As late as 1980, two-thirds of all the world's households living in absolute poverty were still in the rural areas of the developing countries; by the year 2000, more than half will be located in the cities. And, overall, if the present trend continues, more than 60 percent of the world's population increase will take place in the urban areas. Not surprisingly, then, fueled as it is by the volatile mixture of population and poverty, the fallout generated by the urban explosion is changing the map of the Third World.

FIVE

The cumulative effect of the communications revolution of this past century—movies, radio, and now television—cannot be discounted; it doubtless played a prime role in helping to light the two fuses. But more than that, it touched off what has been called "an aspiration explosion" of its own. Certainly, it intensified a rural consciousness that there is an urban alternative to traditional ways of existence. Economic displacement as agriculture changes its modes of production, the fabled excitement of the big city, the urban bias of the national planning of many a new Third World country anxious to industrialize and hence to keep city food costs below that of the countryside—all these factors and more certainly come into play. But above all is the idea that the city represents opportunity—opportunity of employment, opportunity to better one's status. This is the mystic dimension, the prime catalyst of Third World migration to the city, and then the glue that keeps the migrants there no matter what they must endure.

The numbers have been described as traumatic, a human tidal wave that caught the cities unprepared. Mexico City, for one, is overwhelmed by slums and shantytowns that, when put together, are larger than the Federal District itself. But the Mexico City seen by the outside world and the one seen by those seeking refuge there are two different cities. The pollution, the traffic, the slums, the pavements, the shantytowns—even a lean-to made of packing crates set on "Mount Dump," one of the many rising mountains of garbage that now ring the city—all that seems easier to put up with than what was left behind.

A pavement dweller squatting on Bombay's hovel-lined Reay Road says, "Not to have come here would have meant starvation . . . This may not be much, but at least there is a chance things may get better." The words change from city to city, but the theme is always the same: There is a new urban alternative to the old rural—and hopeless—way of existence.

So while it may sound contradictory, the abysmal living conditions that are now a way of life for the majority in the cities of the Third World are not an accurate barometer of whether the migrant has, in fact, improved his lot. Housing is low on the list of his priorities, jobs are at the top. If that means the pavement in Bombay, a swamp in Lagos, a mausoleum in Cairo, Mount Dump in Mexico City, so be it.

The siren song of the city is so strong, not even out and out disaster—or the imminent threat of one—can discourage the migrants. Certainly, not many were frightened off by the deadly earthquakes that struck Mexico City in 1985, and no one seemed to pack up and go back to the countryside after the devastating mudslides that, early in 1985, smashed through the *favelas,* the shantytowns where three million people live precariously perched on the steep slopes surrounding Rio de Janeiro. Be it in Mexico, Brazil, or any other developing country where disaster has signaled what may be in store for other cities ill-prepared and ill-equipped to cope with the floods inundating them, the people come anyway. Whatever the dangers of the unknown that await them, insofar as they are concerned, the greater danger is the one they know—the barren, hopeless countryside.

For most, however, the rural poverty that is their baggage is perpetuated in the city. The jobs they came for are few and, if they find any, poorly paid; malnutrition is rife; housing is the worst the city can offer. A little more than a decade ago, with the explosion well-underway, Barbara Ward gave this graphic account:

> Millions upon millions crowded in the exploding cities, all too often without the minimal provisions for urban cleanliness, offer man's most concentrated insult to the support systems of air, water, and soil upon whose integrity the survival of life itself depends.

Little has changed, except that with tens of millions more now at risk, the insult is even greater. And added to it all, the conditions in which they live have exposed the migrants to a whole host of infectious diseases, such as tuberculosis, thought to have been all but eliminated; and they have become easy prey for new plagues, such as AIDS, for which the cures, if any, are yet to be found.

Why, then, do they keep coming? One answer is they have nothing to lose. Also, a few do make it and just knowing that is enough to keep hope alive and the roads filled. Aptly enough, the entire phenomenon has been dubbed "the Las Vegas effect," with the migrants likened to gamblers flocking to some huge casino, or buying tickets in a vast lottery, understanding full well the odds are stacked against them, but hoping against hope that lightning will strike.

This lure is nothing new. It dates back almost to the origin of the city itself, especially to the world's greatest cities. We become so immersed in their mythic qualities, Bombay architect and city planner Charles Correa says, we do not always see their physical reality.

> If you were to visit Manhattan, but could not feel or comprehend its myths . . . what would you see? [he asks.] A monotonous grid of traffic intersections and buildings like pigeonholes, much like Cleveland, Detroit, and a dozen other North American cities. But Fifth Avenue . . . Central Park . . . Forty-second Street . . . the very names are magic! We do not hear them for what they really are— mere numbers on a map, planners' shorthand. They have become the stuff of which dreams are made. So also with the burgeoning metropolis of the Third World. What to the outside may appear as a mere mass of humanity, spreading in all directions to infinity, to the people themselves could well be a place of unique opportunity, with truly mystic dimensions.

So the deluge goes on, and cities are racing to catch up—a race that many of them are running on a treadmill. The faster they run, the more they do to catch up, the faster they must run, the more they need to do, as more and more rural refugees pour into them. With no letup in sight, by the time the twenty-first century passes its first quarter, the cities of the Third World will be the overcrowded, congested home of nearly four billion people, the poor, the homeless, the pavement dwellers, the slum- and shantytown-confined, the inadvertent, accidental pioneers of the new urban world.

SIX

The outlook is bleak and discouraging. But it would be a mistake to predict disaster as the inevitable outcome. That does not take into account such intangibles as the human spirit; nor does it reckon with human ingenuity. The danger is great, and getting greater every day, but a start is being made as some cities, rather than wait for disaster to strike, search to see how matters can be managed, even with the unparalleled growth that literally has them bursting at their seams.

New investigations into the cycles of life and development inside the shantytowns, for example, are not just looking for a quick-fix, Band-Aid solution; increasingly, they are looking to the long term. For the undeniable fact is that the shantytowns, already expanding at twice the rate of the cities themselves, and with untold millions more headed to them, simply cannot be wished or willed away. The reality is they will be around for a long time to come, and the choice is between seeing them proliferate as modern-day infernos, or taking steps that will absorb them into the daily life of the cities to which they are attached. Like it or not, the number of shantytown dwellers is such that without them (and the source of cheap labor they provide), more than one city's economy would be in trouble.

Meanwhile, there seems to a growing appreciation of what may, or may not, work in limiting urban growth. Efforts to prevent rural immigration by interdiction, carrot or stick, simply have not been successful, whether transferring the migrants back to the countryside or making the city off limits to them entirely, as Djkarta and Manila once tried and failed. Nor, as Bombay and Calcutta learned, will forcibly removing squatters from the pavement keep them from coming back (a lesson being learned in New York, too, albeit on a microscopic scale). Even in cities where government control is more efficient in holding down movement, real patent costs are surfacing and getting a second look.

Much more than in the past, moreover, there is a growing recognition, both in the developing and in the industrialized countries, that it is the city that will be the testing ground for many of the profound social, economic, and political changes that the new century has in store for us. It is there, in the city, that the world will have to learn to cope as never before with education and unemployment; with management of the environment and of natural resources too often taken for granted, like air and water; with control of pollution and traffic and waste; with how to ensure housing, health, and welfare in concentrations of unparalleled density; and with a score and more of related and interlocking issues now demanding their rightful place on the global agenda.

But given their volatile growth and the direct bearing it has on their immediate future, few issues on that agenda are more important to the cities bearing the brunt of the explosion than the outcome of policies to reduce their population growth. As the wealthier industrialized world discovered in past generations, and as the poorer countries are finding out today, the factors closely associated with urban culture—literacy, better health services, greater job opportunities, an improvement in the status of women—can in time help lower birth rates.

With their populations growing three and four times as fast as Europe in its heyday, however, the developing countries do not have the same time to wait, and most of them are now actively trying to encourage national voluntary family-planning programs. In doing so, they have come a long way from the stand they were taking less than a generation ago when they viewed population efforts of any kind as part of a western plot designed to keep them weak and subjugated. Today, even Third World countries with predominantly Catholic populations have done an about-face, and lower fertility rates are looked upon as essential not only to defuse the urban explosion, but to assure the success of their overall economic development programs and the fight against poverty.

The great dilemma they face is that change will be slow, and as things stand now, it is still hard to see any light at the end of the tunnel. Outside of China, only a limited number of people (in Africa, for example, it is less than 10 percent) have access to family-planning services and contraceptives, or to the education and information needed to make use of them. A World Fertility Survey (a social science study conducted in 41 developing countries) put the number of women thus affected at 250 million. That number is significant just by itself, but it is even more revealing seen in the light of other studies showing that when women are given a chance to make choices about their futures, and also given enough education to seize that chance, most of them invariably decide in favor of smaller families.

That, at least, has been the experience in developing countries in which effective family-planning programs have had a clear impact on the birth rate. But the drop is still far too small to change the overall growth of global population. It continues to go up, with consequences that will range well beyond the urban explosion itself. For the more people there are in the world, the greater the demand on an already fragile and overloaded ecosystem on which all life depends. From the air that we breathe to the water we drink to the land that feeds us, the earth may be reaching the limit of what it can absorb in the way of human interference. It is a threat now to be found deep in our oceans, in far-off rain forests and distant mountains, and even high in the atmosphere, where a greenhouse effect could turn the earth into a hothouse. And most visible to us because we are surrounded by it every day is the evidence we see in our cities: In the industrialized countries, we see them producing massive, uncontrolled amounts of waste and pollutants; and in the developing countries, we see them, bulging and sprawling, more often than not following in the same dangerous footsteps.

But the rush to the city goes on as before (the Worldwatch Institute calls it the dominant demographic trend of the late twentieth century, aside from population growth itself). And when population growth stabilizes a hundred years from now, as the United Nations Population Fund expects that it will, the rural areas will be largely deserted, and at least 75 percent of all the people then on earth will be massed in cities and urban centers of all sizes. Compared to the urban world that will come into being at the end of the twentieth century, that will be a mega-jump of at least 25 percent.

A close-up satellite picture of the earth is said to look, conversely, like a view from earth into the depth of space, with the stars, nebulae, and galaxies making up the cities—urban constellations, as it were, glowing against a deep, dark background. One image the description suggests reflects the importance of our cities here on earth shining as centers of human attraction, intellectual light, and economic power. It is a bright picture, in sum, of a civilization and planet with the creative and technological capacity to forge the greatest social transformation in history.

But then there is the image suggested by the blackness surrounding the cities. Its depth and extent can be seen as the darkness formed by the dehumanizing slums and shantytowns, no less than the shameful poverty, the inequality, the discrimination that now make up the urban ghettos of the world. Until these are dealt with, no transformation is possible, and we face the real danger of the darkness reaching into the brightness of the cities themselves, making them bare bases of survival. And if that should be this century's heritage to the next, it would be a denial of history and a tragedy we cannot begin to contemplate.

For now, it is hard to see through the fallout. When the dust settles, there will be a new urban order, unplanned and unintended, and perhaps the answer will be found somewhere in between the extremes.

THE
CITIES

MEXICO CITY

Its mayor bluntly calls Mexico City a paradox of extreme modernity and heartrending underdevelopment. The reason is not hard to find in a city that has multiplied itself forty-five times over in this century alone and is now the largest urban agglomeration the world has ever known.

Gloomy prophets warn of a Malthusian apocalypse unless the city's growth is curbed, and most Mexicans agree something must be done. For all the fierce pride they have in their country's capital, they are painfully aware that the 1985 earthquake's excessive toll of dead, injured, and homeless was only partly due to its violence, that by far the greater number of casualties came from the serious congestion in the inner city, one of the most densely populated places in the world. Insofar as they are concerned, therefore, the "largest city" title is a curse, and they would rather be rid of it.

Juarez, Mexico's first President, still keeps watch

A city of contrasts: Mother and daughters in Netzahualcóyotl . . .

The Mexico City of today had its roots in the ancient Aztec capital of Tenochtitlán, already a thriving, sophisticated metropolis nearly five hundred years ago, when it was destroyed by the Spanish conquistadors. Rebuilt on the ruins, the city grew slowly, starting the century with barely 400,000 people, its streets tranquil and unhurried, its air clear, the craggy mountain peaks and volcanoes that tower well above the 7000-foot-high plateau it straddles etched sharply against a deep-blue sky.

By the time Mexico City leapfrogged past Tokyo as the world's largest city in 1986, its population was 18 million and climbing. Its downtown streets were a tangle of teeming humanity and screaming traffic, its once pure air a respiratory menace, and the magnificence of its natural setting shrouded in a murky, polluted smog. Not much change is expected by the end of the century, except that the city's population will then be 26 million, according to government estimates. (The World Bank talks in terms of 31 million, and unofficial projections are even higher.)

Whatever its population in 2000, everyone agrees it is more than the city can adequately deal with right now. The oil boom of the 1970s gave momentary hope that Mexico's economy was on the upswing. But when the bubble burst, it gave new impetus to a "distress" migration of rural *campesinos*, fleeing either outward to the United States border or inward to the industrialized cities of the country. At the height of it all, Mexico City was getting as many as a thousand refugees a day. The reasons are not hard to come by.

. . . and wealthy riders on a quiet street

Mexico City is the country's capital and its largest city. It houses 90 percent of the government's machinery and most of its bureaucracy. It contains more than half of Mexico's total industrial plants. It is the hub of Mexican finance and commerce, the heart of its academic, cultural, and intellectual life, and just about any other activity or initiative of consequence.

Downtown traffic

A curbside job market

It is not surprising then that Mexico City has become the home of one in five Mexicans, nor that the flow continues even though jobs are scarce, affordable housing all but nonexistent, and prices and day-to-day living costs inflated beyond the ability of most to keep up with. Described as "the capital of underdevelopment" by novelist Carlos Fuentes, it remains, in spite of all its troubles, one of the world's great cities, parts of it still among the most beautiful. Its explosion has dimmed some of the luster, but not the underlying grandeur.

A dramatically modern skyline designed by some of the world's leading contemporary architects makes for a striking contrast with a proud Spanish colonial heritage. Mixed in with the old, the new, and the grand, however, is the unmistakable mark of the explosion; the makeshift shacks thrown together from cardboard, plastic, tin; the broken-down *viendados;* the slums; the shantytowns that, all combined, are larger than the Federal District, with millions (some say more than half the city's total population) crammed into what is euphemistically called "irregular" housing.

Garbage pickers sell what they can cull

The city itself is now actually a divided urban sprawl of some 1250 square miles, roughly half in the Federal District (the old city and seat of the government) and the other half in outlying districts of two neighboring states, once an area of expensive suburbs and exurbs. Together, the two halves make up a rambling metropolitan area, its outskirts—in essence bedroom communities for the city's industrial and governmental bureaucracies—blanketed by shantytowns that run for miles in all directions. One of the shantytowns, Netzahualcóyotl, has itself become a virtual city of three million, a mix of migrants both from the countryside and from inside the Federal District. (There, sharply rising rents and land values have created refugees of their own, the urban refugees driven from an inner city they no longer can afford.)

Slum in the shadow of a skyscraper

The morning gridlock "market" in the Federal District

The tortured lines of traffic on the roads leading into the Federal District in the morning—and then the other way at night—attest to an influx greater than the available housing, or water, or sewage, or even streets. And things are not much better inside the District, with parts of it having one of the highest density ratios to be found anywhere.

The crowds are hard to escape. Buses and subways are packed, and a Sunday stroll in Chapultepec Park, one of the few remaining green spaces, can be a weekday rush-hour experience, with uncounted thousands of homeless and peddlers adding to the congestion in the streets. But the crowds are relaxed, and fire-eaters blow flames into the night at major intersections where stalled traffic provides captive audiences.

Fire-eater entertaining in a traffic jam

Life in Mexico City—in shantytown and Federal District alike—is hard for most, and turning things around will not be easy. The immediate priority is to slow the pace of the city's growth, making it, as its mayor says, more controlled and more orderly. Migrants are encouraged to settle in other Mexican cities, and incentives are being offered to industries, particularly the heavy polluters, to induce them to relocate elsewhere.

On and off, there is talk of decentralizing the government itself by moving some of the vast bureaucracy to other cities, and there is no shortage of other plans and programs. But it will take years before the returns are in, and in any event, the key to the future of the city is the future of the country's economy, and that will be a difficult struggle at best. Tied in with it is the parallel effort to lower the rate of the

Newborn "assembly line"

Large families—the heritage of religion and tradition

country's population growth, which perhaps is the biggest paradox of all in this capital of a predominantly Catholic country in which large families are the custom both because of religion and tradition.

"It's a matter of survival for us" is the pragmatic explanation given by one of the architects of the program. "We are opposed to the concept of demographic fatalism."

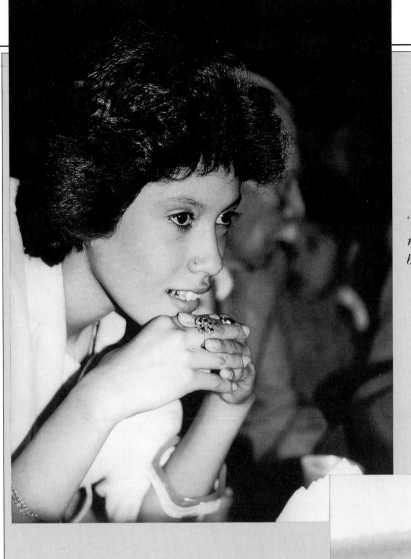

"I want to see [Mexico City] grow not in size and in people, but in beauty and opportunity. . . ."

"Mexico City is a paradox . . . where the extremes of modernity are juxtaposed with heartrending underdevelopment . . . [and] where a dignified and stable coexistence among its inhabitants is very difficult. . . . Our most important priority now is to control our future growth. . . ."
—Mayor Ramón Aguirre Velasquez

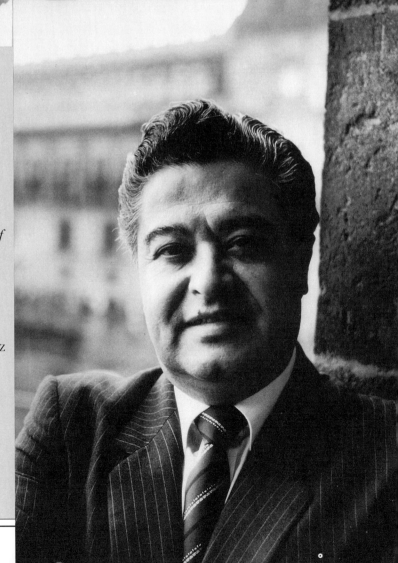

Coordinated by a government-sponsored national population council, family-planning programs are supported and made available to the public in youth and community centers, schools, hospitals and clinics and through other public and private initiatives. Since 1970, the rate of population growth has dropped from 3.5 percent to 2 percent.

Overall, population in Mexico now stands at 80 million, with government projections estimating that it will reach 100 million by the year 2000, well below previous estimates. And if this really turns out to be the case, Mexico City's population should, in fact, not go above 26 million in 2000, still more than any other city in the world, but decidedly better than the 36 million predicted for it not so long ago.

However, this goal still remains more of a hope than any firm expectation. For while Mexico City's birthrate shows signs of going down, its overall population keeps going up as new immigrants arrive every day, undaunted by the problems they know await them and drawn by a force almost mystic in the power it exerts.

The old city

CAIRO

The desert sky is still dark when Cairo comes awake. Its narrow, twisting roads and streets quickly fill and throb with life and activity, and none of them more than in the City of the Dead where half a million people live in the shadow of the barren Muqattam mountain range, surrounded by some of the most impressive Islamic monuments in the world.

Women walking to market

Cairo's explosion has left it with more than ten million people, five times the number the city originally was designed to hold. During the day, at least three million commuters from outlying suburbs also squeeze into the Egyptian capital. They come by foot, bus, tram, car, truck, bicycle, and donkey cart; traffic is so intense as it approaches Tahrir Square, the heart of Cairo and the center of a spiderweb of streets and roads, that everything moving—pedestrians at times included—merges into a massive gridlock.

The morning squeeze into Cairo

Gridlock and construction: two familiar sights

Sphinx and pyramid at Giza

Crowded street in central Cairo

Adding to the congestion and lending a bewildered, frenzied look to the scene is the widespread construction underway everywhere, particularly in the downtown area: new buildings going up, old ones being repaired, mosques and monuments being restored, water and sewage pipes going down, a subway (Cairo's first) being built. The massive equipment, the detours, the excavations—all contribute to an appearance of a city anxiously trying to catch up with itself—and with the twentieth century.

The past is never far away. Appearing in a reddish haze on the edge of the desert, its outskirts rising abruptly where the arid, dusty land leaves off, Cairo stands on the banks of the storied river Nile. Both pyramid and skyscraper cast their shadows in its waters, their shimmering images reflecting the uneasy struggle now going on between the city's thousand-year-old past and its emerging present. Symbolic of it in a way are the archaeologists, who serve as members of the construction crews working on the city's subway and water and sewerage projects. It is one of the reasons why the work is painfully slow. Every shovelful dug up must be carefully sifted—it may be rich in history.

Children living in a garbage dump

The haze that hangs over Cairo much of the time smarts the eyes and sears the lungs. Not even the desert winds are enough to disperse the heavy, lingering bumper-to-bumper automobile exhaust that mixes in the heart of the city with the noxious, acrid fumes drifting in from zinc and lead smelters in the northern suburbs and cement and steel plants to the south.

Half a million people lived in Cairo when the twentieth century started; today it has more than twenty times as many. And the explosion still goes on, with some 350,000 people being added to the population every year, half of them rural immigrants seeking work they cannot find in other parts of a country in which only three percent of the land is arable. At this rate, the expectation is that by the end of the century, Cairo will be jammed with a population of at least 16 million, and possibly many more.

Available apartments are few, the people many

The presence of so many people has obliterated any lines of demarcation between Cairo and nearby towns and created a sprawling metropolitan area known as Greater Cairo. An inner core that up to the nineteenth century consisted of less than three square miles has burst, overrunning farms and pastures, and the region covers more than 1800 square miles, extending westward across the Nile all the way to Giza and the pyramids. In some sections, the population density is said to run as high as 300,000 people per square mile, and stucco and brick buildings are so pressed together, the sun barely shines through; while the buildings themselves—five, six, and seven stories high—are filled to overflowing with what some estimate to be just about half of Cairo. Demands for added water and sewage lines have not been able to keep pace, and often it is necessary to pick one's way carefully through old cobblestone streets and dirt roads waiting to be paved.

For all of its run-down housing and poverty—Egypt is one of the poorest countries in the Middle East—Cairo is also a city of luxury and wealth, with gracious old estates and glittering new high rises. Many longtime Cairenes are unhappy over what they see as the "ruralification" of the city, and believe that its future may be threatened unless the government embarks on an intensive effort to urbanize the countryside itself. But no one is quite sure how this could be accomplished in a country in which the big urban centers—Cairo and Alexandria—already suffer a serious shortage of jobs.

Not even that shortage, however, is enough to discourage the rural refugees; nor are they put off by the repeated crises that are sure to erupt every day in one part of the city or another: water pipes burst; sewage lines back up; public transportation breaks down. Up and down the line, the city urgently needs the new infrastructure it is now trying to build. The World Bank and the French and American governments are helping with the water and sewage systems and the construction of the new subway, and there is hope that when these are finished the city will have taken a long step toward the twenty-first century. There is also hope that by then a new road system, including a ring road on the outskirts, will help to unsnarl the city's traffic.

Everyone agrees housing is Cairo's major problem. Several public-housing projects are underway, but construction is way behind the actual need. And most of what does come on the market is priced below the reach of all but the wealthy, so the shortage grows year by year, together with the population. The result today is that nearly all the city's poor live in substandard housing, 35 percent of which the government says is so old or so far gone, not even rehabilitation would make it safe for occupancy. And as if to emphasize the point, every now and then one of the houses suddenly collapses, another sign of the struggle between the past and the present: The city's underground water table is shifting because of the tunnels being dug for the new subway, literally the last straw for many of the older building foundations.

Millions—an exact number is hard to come by—have thus turned to "informal housing," which covers just about 80 percent of all the construction now going on. "Informal" here means without authorization, and it ranges from squatter shacks for rural migrants in a garbage dump to modern new high-rise residential and office buildings in which the government itself rents hard-to-get space. Not unusual, too, is the piggybacking of one- or two-story additions on existing rooftops.

"Satellite" city being built in the desert

Cairo's housing problems, however, have not given rise to the vast shantytowns of the kind so common in other cities of the developing world. This is due in part to what some have called a self-mobilizing kind of energy on the part of its people to improve conditions for themselves. The City of the Dead, which falls in the informal-housing category, is perhaps one of the best examples of this energy at work.

A misnomer—not one but several cemeteries are involved—the City of the Dead is by no means a new addition to the Cairo scene. Indeed, its use by the living goes back for decades, and what started out as a movement by squatters has now become a well-entrenched community. Squatters still keep coming in, but so does a wide range of Cairo society—civil servants, shopkeepers, laborers, professionals. They are philosophical about their surroundings, most of them overcoming their qualms and moving to the City of the Dead because its aboveground burial vaults and graveside shelters (originally built as rest houses for visitors) are just about the best value around.

The waiting list is long, and those lucky enough to get in are envied as being more fortunate than most. An unofficial but efficient network of cemetery workers (a local wag has dubbed it Cairo's "underground real estate combine") keeps tabs on availability, with successful applicants either renting or purchasing the tombs or shelters outright, the same as they would an apartment or house in any other Cairo neighborhood.

By this time, the City of the Dead has its own shopping centers, bus lines and other utilities service it, and small businesses and industries have sprung up here and there. Children playing soccer or skipping rope, even as on any city street, are not unusual sights. Neither is a television antenna poking its way above a mausoleum. The City of the Dead, in short, is an established fact of Cairo life. It is also a measure of its dilemma.

Looking ahead, Cairo has embarked on an ambitious program aimed at funneling people out of its congested inner core and spreading them into new cities and satellite communities being built on the outskirts and in the desert itself. The biggest hurdle that must be overcome here is convincing enough people to leave the inner city and move into the new settlements. There has been some movement, but for the most part the new settlements still have a frontier look about them, and even enthusiastic proponents of the scheme recognize that a mass movement into the desert is not a realistic hope, at least not immediately. Overcrowded though it is in the inner core, few want to leave if the choice is up to them.

Meanwhile, new immigrants and new babies keep the city's population soaring, a reflection of what is happening in a country that is growing by one million people every eight months. Five years ago, a baby was born every 27 seconds; by 1987, one was being born every

21 seconds. And with 43 percent of the population still under fifteen, some 200,000 more people are reaching reproductive age every year, an anticipated impact on the future birthrate that had the government itself issue a sobering projection suggesting the possibility of Egypt's population—now at 49 million—doubling every 25 years.

New life in the City of the Dead

Soccer among the mausoleums

"... I want to finish school so I can be a teacher and help with the changes we must bring about in our city and country...."

"... The manifestations of modernity, the increased human traffic between the southern and the northern parts of the country, the population explosion, and a host of military and economic conditions are all exacting their toll ... the satisfactory solution [of our problems] will depend to a great extent on our ability to recognize and utilize all our existing potential to meet our existing needs, and at the same time maintain our cherished traditions...."

—Governor Youssef Sabry Abu-Taleb

Coming to terms with reality involves religion, culture, and tradition, all powerful forces that have long made family planning a particularly sensitive subject in Egypt. It still is, but it is now also a top priority in Cairo, considered so important both to the city's and to the country's future that the President of Egypt serves as the chairman of a National Family Planning Council to coordinate a government-sponsored program promoting the use of various forms of contraception. Schools, clinics, and other community groups and organizations are involved in the effort, with birth-control devices either distributed free or available at subsidized prices. Young couples are also being urged to increase the "spacing" between children, and older women past thirty-five to have fewer children or none at all because of the health risks that may be involved. And, although this is not part of the program, the birthrate may also be affected by the fact that in overcrowded Cairo it's not easy for newly married couples to set up housekeeping in a place all their own.

The ultimate goal for the country is a growth rate of 2.1 percent, a national goal whose achievement is regarded as essential if Egypt is to solve its economic malaise. For Cairo, the hope is that the city's problems will then begin to abate as well, although that day is off in the distant future. Certainly, through to the end of the century and well into the next, the City of the Dead will be overrun with the living.

Shanghai Harbor: China's window on the world

SHANGHAI

Less than half a century ago, Shanghai was a freewheeling, wealthy city envied by the rest of China and known in the West as "the wildest seaport" on the face of the earth. There is a vast difference now. One of the biggest of the twentieth century's breed of giant metropolises, Shanghai's lurid past never really prepared it for the role it plays today as a bridge between China and the rest of the world.

Actually, Shanghai is an exception among cities of the Third World. Its explosion is behind it.

With 12 million people, Shanghai is China's largest and most congested city, its major seaport handling the lion's share of trade with more than 150 countries. It is also China's industrial, commercial, and financial capital; the headquarters for a growing number of private enterprises, both domestic and international; and one of the country's leading educational and cultural centers.

But for all the many important roles it already plays, and before all the grand plans for its future can be realized (work has been started to bring it into the computer and informational network), Shanghai has a lot of catching up to do.

When the British opium fleet steamed into it in the early nineteenth century, Shanghai was a minor fishing port at a junction of the Huangpu River and Suzhou Creek, where the rich Yangtze Basin

Computer education is a new priority for Shanghai's future

Shanghai crowds and traffic equal China's most congested city

The city's changing skyline: run-down older buildings mingle with modern skyscrapers

empties into the East China Sea (from which, legend has it, the city actually emerged, its name literally meaning "up from the sea"). Soon after the British arrived, the place took on the racy reputation that was to endure until the end of World War II. Today, it is hard to reconcile "the wildest seaport" with a city more than a little frayed at the edges, its streets old and sedate, its buildings run-down and bare, its population graying, its youth at a premium.

Once envied by other Chinese who likened the city to the Emperor's ugly daughter with no worries about ever finding a suitor, Shanghai today is trying to live down its past. Its heritage from the days it was a treaty port are not much of a help. For more than a hundred years, the city was divided into the Chinese Area, the International Settlement, and the French Concession, with the foreign enclaves so busy capitalizing on the access their foothold gave them into China's interior, that—their own enclaves aside—they had little time for the city itself. All in all, prior to the Communist takeover in 1949, not much was done to plan Shanghai's development as a major international center. And even after 1949, other priorities always seemed to interfere, with the subsequent Cultural Revolution cutting deep into the city's industrial heart and adding to its already growing urban problems.

But nothing interfered with the city's growth. Five million people were already vying for space in 1949, a number that more than doubled in little more than a generation as Shanghai turned into an overcrowded, underhoused city with a creaky old infrastructure. That the sewage line of one of the old enclaves, for example, had never been intended to fit into the line of another may be a Trivial Pursuit fact of history, but it also helps explain some of the troubles Shanghai has come up against in creating a smoothly running, up-to-date city. And given Shanghai's importance to the Chinese economy as a whole, its problems have extended well beyond any traditional city limits.

In terms of sheer physical size—which is huge by any standard—the Shanghai metropolitan region today is not much larger than it was in 1949. Sprawling over roughly 4000 square miles, it is divided into a relatively small inner core and a large outer shell running well into the surrounding countryside. Despite the two cores' discrepancy in size, the population is about equally divided between them, creating congestion in the small inner city that some reports put at nearly half a million people in each square mile.

New construction is only now beginning to make its presence seen and felt, but it has a long way to go before it changes the prevailing European design: broad avenues and boulevards and Continental-style buildings. Indeed, Nanjing Road, the main shopping area that is never empty, and the Bund, the storied waterfront district where the European banks and trading houses flourished, have changed so little in terms of their outward physical appearance, they have been described by those who knew Shanghai before the war as "frozen in time."

The European-built Bund, "frozen in time"

Tai Chi Chuan, *a dawn ritual*

Boats on the Huangpu leaving the city . . .

. . . and millions of commuters bicycling in

The city's air of nostalgia is particularly evident in the early-morning dawn, when row upon row of gray-clad, silent men and women gather in the Bund. There, and in streets all over the city, as light begins to break, they engage in the ancient ritual of *Tai Chi Chuan,* looking for all the world like some mass corps de ballet shadow boxing in slow motion. Meanwhile, the crowds on Nanjing Road start building up—by early afternoon they will merge into an almost solid mass—while on the river, boats move through the rising mist: sampans, houseboats, ferries, oceangoing freighters, all sounding their foghorns. And wave after wave of bicycle-riding commuters—some two million of them—launch their daily invasion from the outskirts.

The bicycle remains one of the main means of transportation in a city where public transport is both old and in short supply. With private cars a luxury, taxis few and far between, and buses old and overloaded, the bicycle is the true vehicle of the people, the cause of many a traffic jam, and the most serious menace a pedestrian must dodge.

Shanghai's first subway is expected to open in 1990

But change is in the air—or rather, underground—as Shanghai gets ready for its first subway. The initial shafts have gone down, the tunnels and stations are well advanced, and the first of seven lines is expected to be in operation before 1990.

Among the other priorities city officials talk about are new streets and roads, the rebuilding and expansion of the water and sewage systems (funded with the help of the World Bank), a new bridge over the Huangpu River to link the two sides of Shanghai now connected mainly by ferries, and the re-equipping and restructuring of factories, many of them bravely chugging along with old machinery.

No one questions Shanghai's needs. The question—an echo of the one being asked in virtually every other city—is how to pay for what must be done. Shanghai's earnings—its ports, its textile, electronics, and other industries—provides about one-sixth of China's state revenues, all of it badly needed to help pay for the country's overall modernization program. But Shanghai's income has gone down in the last few years. And while Beijing is now making it easier for the city to compete in the free market, and is also siphoning back a larger share of the revenue, with everything that must be done to bring an old, decaying infrastructure up to date, it still is not enough.

And if rapidly rising social costs and housing, too, are included, the city faces some difficult days, a fact its officials are among the first to acknowledge. Just to take housing, Shanghai has no slums or shantytowns, nor, for that matter, any homeless problems. But much of its housing is old and shabby, badly in need of repair and modernizing. (Because of the lack of both space and equipment, in some sections it is not unusual for household chores—cooking, laundry, and the like—to be done on the street.) The overall shortage—the average per capita living space is 13 square feet—makes sharing by families a way of life, especially in the inner city, where the assignment of apartments is strictly controlled by committees in the neighborhood and the workplace. Rarely, if ever, does a young couple get to live alone; rather, the norm is two- and three-generation households, and little change is expected in this century at least.

Shanghai's aging face

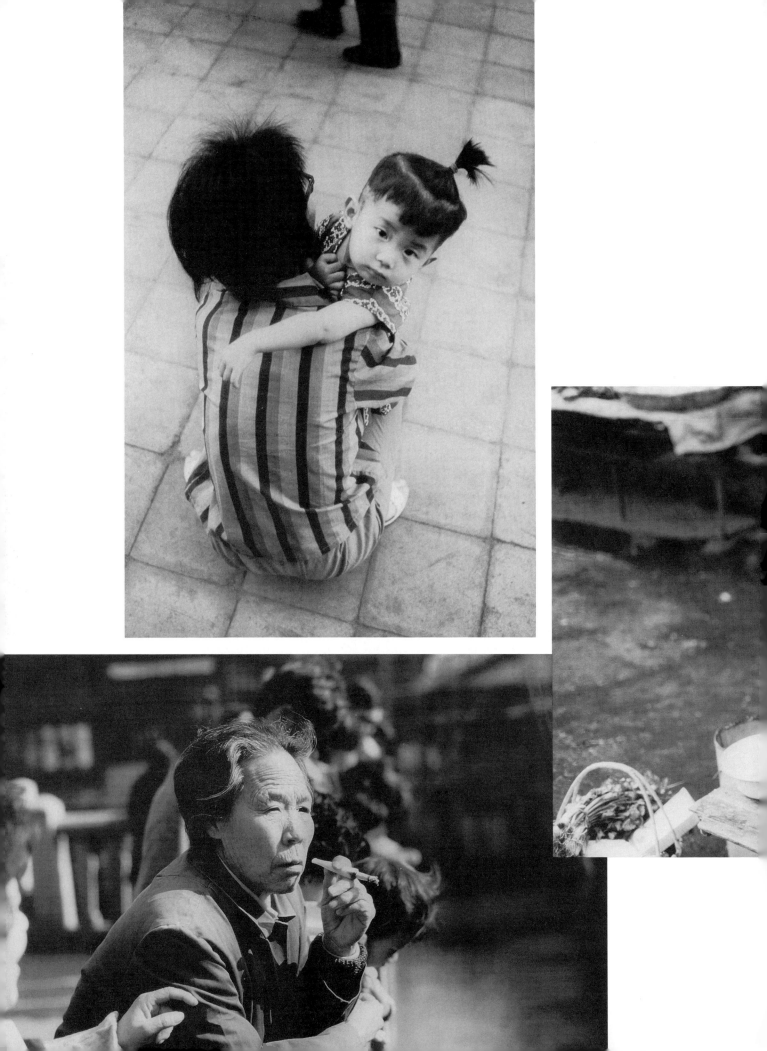

China's national family policy: one child per family . . .

City authorities estimate they move some 48,000 to 70,000 families to new apartments every year. But that is far from enough; it is the equivalent, as one official ruefully described it, of trying to make progress by walking slowly on a fast treadmill.

To help ease the situation, seven satellite cities have been developed, built around steel plants, metallurgical factories, scientific research institutions, and automobile assembly plants. The hope is that by the year 2000, the program will have provided jobs and apartments for at least a million people, including those who will live in new projects planned in the bay area.

But these projects, as well as virtually everything else in Shanghai, will be affected in the new century by the city's steadily aging population, an unexpected turn of events attributable to two unrelated developments. One is the now discredited Cultural Revolution of the 1970s that forced many young people out of the city to work in the countryside. The other is the Beijing government's national family-planning policy instituted in 1979 to help slow the growth of a country that today has topped one billion and is now the most populous in the world.

The policy, which aims at a 1.0 percent fertility rate, encourages both late marriages and then only one child per family; and the Chinese population is beginning to show its impact, one particularly marked in Shanghai. With a birthrate already reflecting the Cultural Revolution-inspired exodus of people who were then in their childbearing years, the number of the city's young today has dwindled, even as the number of its aged has grown. The two will soon be out of balance. Looking ahead to the year 2000, the Shanghai Social Science Academy warns that by then the over-sixty population—already approaching 1.5 million—will shoot way up, with those sixty-five and older comprising more than 14 percent of the total; and then—unless there is a change—their number will more than double, to reach 30 percent by 2025. ("You're never too old to learn," has become the slogan for many of Shanghai's senior citizens; thousands have gone back to school.)

. . . and a sharply reduced birthrate

Re-educating and training the elderly for new skills

One problem its aging poses is that as a major industrial city and seaport, Shanghai urgently needs strong young people to fill jobs on the docks and on the production line. An effort is now being made to build up the service sector, in which age is less of a factor; but 60 percent of all jobs in the city are still industrial, and unless its manpower dilemma is solved, the consequences could complicate Shanghai's revival.

Sixty percent of all jobs in Shanghai are industrial

". . . I am dreaming of becoming a mathematician . . . [So] I can . . . bring benefit to mankind . . . in a world free of war. . . ."

". . . Population is a very important aspect of planning for the future of our city . . . [But] this is problem that cannot be solved by mathematics alone . . . [meanwhile] we must also rebuild the infrastructure of the city, as we are doing . . . [so that] when we begin the new century, the living conditions of our people will be greatly improved compared to today. . . ."

—Mayor Jiang Zemin

Even if China's one child per family policy were to be relaxed in Shanghai, a possible step that has been urged by some in the city, the results would not be apparent until well into the new century. And that would still leave Shanghai with a problem all agree must be solved much sooner than that.

Actually, it has come as no great surprise to most in China that Shanghai should have a unique problem all its own. The other Chinese have traditionally viewed the people in the city as being different, and likewise, the Shanghainese have always thought of themselves as a distinct group—they have their own dialect, not to mention their own special form of opera. And according to an old saying once quoted in Chinese guidebooks, "There is a heaven above, and Saizhou and Hangzhou below. Shanghai is another story . . ."

Within the context of China's overall problems, the same is true today.

City Hall, where the Rome of yesterday mingles with the Rome of today

ROME

Legend once had it that Rome would cease to exist when the gilding disappeared from the two-thousand-year-old bronze equestrian statue of Marcus Aurelius, one of the city's prized archaeological treasures and long considered a symbol of its eternity. The gilding did, in fact, disappear some years ago, eaten away by decades of increasing exposure to corrosive automobile exhaust, but Rome today is flourishing.

Before Rome became Italy's capital in 1870, roughly a quarter of a million people lived in a small part of the area inside the walls originally built by the Emperor Aurelian over seventeen hundred years ago. Today Rome has a population of some 3.5 million people, and the old city is at the core of what has aptly been described as a huge artichoke, spreading open well beyond the perimeter of the ancient walls and out into the surrounding countryside.

Romulus, Remus, and the wolf: the legendary beginnings of Rome

The Coliseum

For all its physical size, however, Rome is one of the most sparsely populated of the world's great cities. With a growth rate that in some of its *circoscrizioni* is close to zero, not much change is likely in the years leading up to the year 2000. Indeed, the expectation is that Rome will enter the new century with no more than four million people, perhaps even fewer, and that the Eternal City will then be an aging city, at least for the foreseeable future.

Historically speaking, Rome is already an old city, dating back more than three thousand years, from the time it was a peaceful pastoral settlement (built, according to tradition, on seven hills) through its centuries as capital of the powerful empire that grew around it. The giver of law and organizer of much of the then-known world, Rome was the source of many of the ideas and techniques of urban development still in use. And even today there exist roads and aqueducts built when Rome was at the height of its glory. Few countries, much less cities, have had such widespread political, cultural, intellectual, and religious impact on the course of civilization.

Overleaf: Repairman and statue, keeping up with the past

Today, that impact may be less powerful. But combining the functions of three cities in one, Rome's influence continues to be felt well out of proportion to its size. It is, first of all, the capital and thus the administrative and political center of Italy; second, it embraces the capital of the Catholic world; and third, it is the home of many of the world's most priceless treasures of art and history.

The Fontana di Trevi, outlet for an aqueduct

With all of Rome's magnificence and beauty—from the Michelangelo-designed Piazza del Campidoglio to the pines of the Villa Borghese, the Forum, the Coliseum, and the many other famed antiquities and edifices—one tends to forget that the city is not just a tourist's paradise. It is also home to the people who live in it. And to them, its beauty and history can be deceptive.

For beyond the confines of historic Rome is a thick urban ring, a mix of modern and shoddy houses, of broad tree-lined avenues and landscaped vistas and pitted and potholed streets and open sewers, some of which still empty into the Tiber. Here is a sharp reminder that Rome is a human city, with many of the everyday problems that less-grand cities face.

At the end of World War II, Rome barely emerged from its surrounding walls, and from any high point one could look out at a stretch of green hills. That view began to disappear in the early 1950s, when what has been called Italy's economic miracle began. Rome then had its own explosion, fueled by an influx of the old Italian peasantry from what was the economically depressed urban desert to the south.

Rome has no really heavy industry—its main industry is its government bureaucracy—but after 1951 there was a spectacular growth in its tertiary service sector, in particular commerce, banking, and transport, with a booming tourist trade that still has not peaked. To top it off, Rome houses an enormous university complex, is the headquarters of a gigantic radio, television, and movie industry, and is one of the world's leading cultural centers. In short, with jobs to be had in Rome, a jobless countryside poured in and population soared.

As one account at the time described it, a "lava-like cement flowed over the green earth, pasture lands gave way to bulldozers and cement apartment-house jungles. . . ." Land values jumped a thousand times as the *borgate,* the outer fringes where suspected political risks were quarantined during the Fascist period, turned into massive suburban bedroom communities. Much of the construction was "illegal," that is, put up by builders who did not bother to do all the paperwork the city required.

Today legal buildings stand side by side with illegal ones, and few know or can tell the difference. Some estimates place the number living in illegal housing at 700,000 to 800,000 people, or one quarter the total population of Rome.

At one point in the immediate post–World War II years, there were, sprinkled in with the luxury housing in the thick urban ring just behind the confines of historic Rome, shacks and shantytowns reminiscent of the exploding cities in the developing world today. Most of these are gone now, but they left a difficult slum-clearance job behind.

The rural areas that once sent people to the cities are economically stronger now, and so Rome is no longer a powerful attraction for immigrants from the countryside. A few still come, but for the most part, Rome's explosion is over. But even at its height, it was a minor explosion compared to the one rocking Third World cities; nonetheless, it redrew the map of the city, and leading Roman urban planners unanimously agree the result bears little resemblance to any logical or desired way for a city to develop.

St. Peter's Square

What happened was that the newer, outer city grew mainly as a place to live, with little in the way of essential services. These remained in the older, inner city, which stayed virtually as it was and which now contains 75 percent of the entire city's social, cultural, administrative, business, and service activities—shopping, schools, hospitals, theaters, and the like, especially the tourist attractions. So every day now, one-quarter of Rome must crisscross the city to get to work, to shop, to go to school. In short, to go anywhere or get anything done in Rome, one-quarter of the city must first run a traffic gauntlet, and then run it again going home.

The long lines of cars, trams, and buses that fill the streets day and night are largely a reflection of all the coming and going to and fro that has become a routine part of Roman life. Also routine now is the resulting exhaust, the same exhaust that a few years ago ate through

Modern Rome's "aqueducts," carrying traffic overhead . . .

. . . and underground

the gilding on the statue of Marcus Aurelius where it stood on its pedestal in Michelangelo's Campidoglio Square. The statue was only one of Rome's many famed antiquities to be damaged by the polluted air, and the city is now in a race against time to save and restore its irreplaceable treasures—the monuments and statues, the fountains, the arches, and the temples.

As a city, Rome's urban concerns focus on unsnarling its traffic (a difficult task in a city in which, according to one observer, obeying traffic rules is "optional" at best); building an "archaeological park" and saving its treasures; bringing order to its housing (one survey says that 400,000 new apartments are badly needed); and a long agenda of other priority programs emerging as the end of the century draws near. Rome is also beginning to pay attention to a situation that is now becoming more and more noticeable: the aging of its population.

Rome, the eternal city, is now an aging city

The trend in Rome is much the same as that in other Western cities: births are down, the mortality rate is down, and people are living longer. Already, those over sixty-five make up 11.5 percent of Rome's population, and by the time the year 2000 is here, with more than half a million, they will comprise 14.3 percent of the total.

The elderly are particularly in evidence in the inner city. There, schools for the young are half-empty, while hospitals treating the elderly are overfilled, as are the few centers that have opened up in recent years to help care for them.

Increasingly heard now are calls for action that will deal with the reality of what is happening. Typical is the view of one demographer: "We need to save our antiquities, it is true [but] even more important, we need to save our old people. . . . They are not as durable as the statues . . . [and] like it or not, Rome will be a city of the aging for a long time to come."

"We worry a lot about terrible things happening in so many countries. . . . We don't want them to happen here. . . ."

"We are linked to history, but Rome cannot just be a museum. . . . We must realize that while we have this magnificent treasure . . . it is not only for us [here in Rome] but for all people everywhere to enjoy. . . . We live with so much splendor, we tend to forget at times that we, as a city, also have problems . . . [and] we must ask ourselves now what kind of a city do we want in the year 2000? We do not have much time to give an answer. . . ."

—Mayor Nicola Signorello

THE URBAN WORLD: A PICTURE ESSAY

Mexico City, Lagos, Cairo, and Bombay are exploding. Shanghai's explosion is behind it, but it is still growing, as is Moscow, and both cities are getting visibly older. New York, Tokyo, and Rome are leveling off, and they, too, are getting older. Third World and industrialized-world cities are, literally, worlds apart in the magnitude and scope of the problems facing them, as well as in the prospects they have for finding solutions in the immediate future. But exploding, leveling off, or growing older, today most cities share certain common concerns, and no one city has been spared the "disamenities" of urban living: crawling lines of traffic, overstuffed commuter trains; congested streets; polluted air; mounting waste; crumbling infrastructures; painful housing shortages; agonizing homelessness. One city has more, another less, but all—no matter what their economy or ideology—have the clearly recognizable signs of today's common urban experience. Never before has it been so universal, at one and the same time so different and so much the same. Babies are born, are loved, nourished, grow. People get married, go to work, go hungry, sleep on the street, are happy, sad, live and die. Here are some of the sights of the city and its people at various stages of the human life cycle, both caught up together in the still ongoing transition that is so radically changing our world and our lives. Here is the composite universal city on the threshold of the urban world.

ONE MINUTE INTO THE EXPLOSION . . .

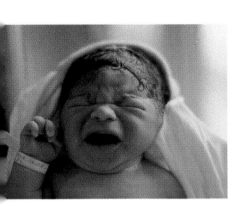

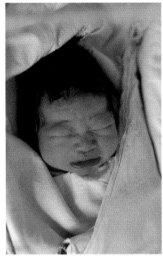

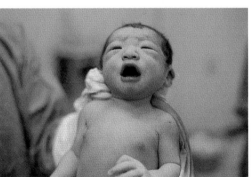

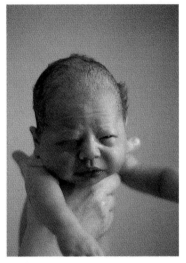

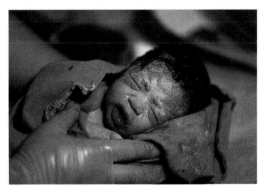

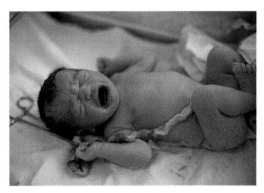

THE CYCLE BEGINS

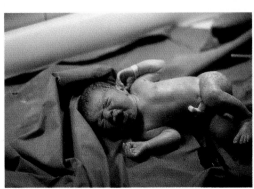

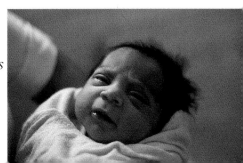

Top row: New York, Shanghai, Lagos
Second row: Tokyo, Moscow
Third row: Mexico City, Cairo
Bottom row: Rome, Bombay

Mosque prayer, Cairo

Lagos (facing page)

Churchgate Station, Bombay

Chapultepec Park, Mexico City

Nanjing Road, Shanghai

Midtown, New York

Haraja-ku, Tokyo

Via Condotti, Rome

Karl Marx Square, Moscow

Bombay (facing page)

THE GLOBAL TRAFFIC JAM

Rome

Cairo

New York

Mexico City

Tokyo

Moscow

New York

THE GLOBAL COMMUTE

Mexico City

Bombay

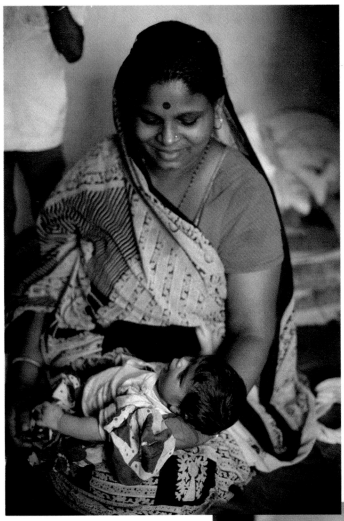

Bombay

Rome

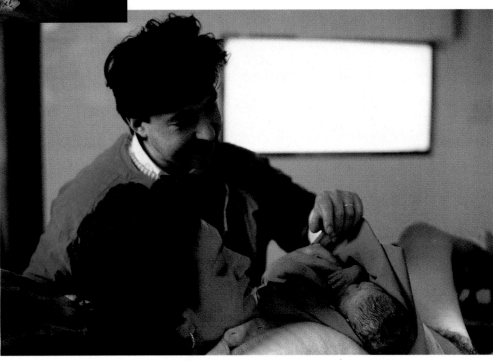

IT'S A SMALL WORLD . . .

Shanghai

Mexico City

Shanghai

Mexico City

Shanghai

Moscow

Moscow

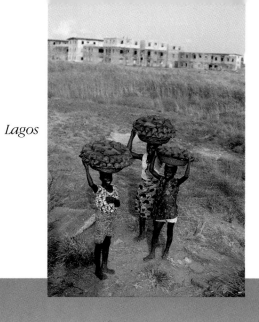

Lagos

Cairo

Shanghai

Rome

Mexico City

Bombay

Bombay

Cairo

New York

New York

...AND GETTING BIGGER

Tokyo

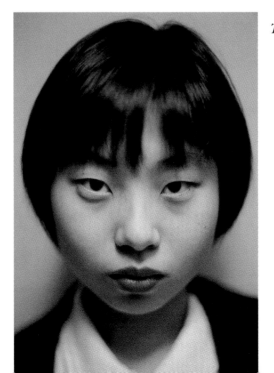

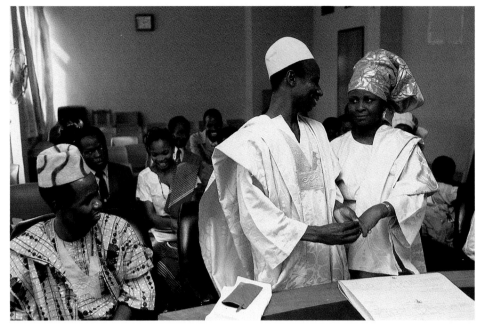

City Hall, Lagos

City Hall, Moscow

Church wedding, Moscow

LOVE AND MARRIAGE

A modern bride- and groom-to-be celebrate, Cairo

Father signing the traditional marriage contract, Cairo

A Roman wedding

Newlyweds and an old tradition, Shanghai

Wedding party, Central Park, New York

A ritual ceremony, Tokyo

*A happy bride,
Mexico City*

A ritual ceremony, Bombay

THE HOMELESS . . .

Inside a squatters' shack, Reay Road, Bombay

"Mt. Dump," Mexico City (facing page)

Squatters' shacks, Lagos

THE POOR . . .

Laundering beside a broken water pipe, Bombay

Squatters' shacks, Bombay

Shack on Mt. Dump, Mexico City

In the courtyard of a slum, Mexico City

Emergency shelter for the homeless, New York (overleaf)

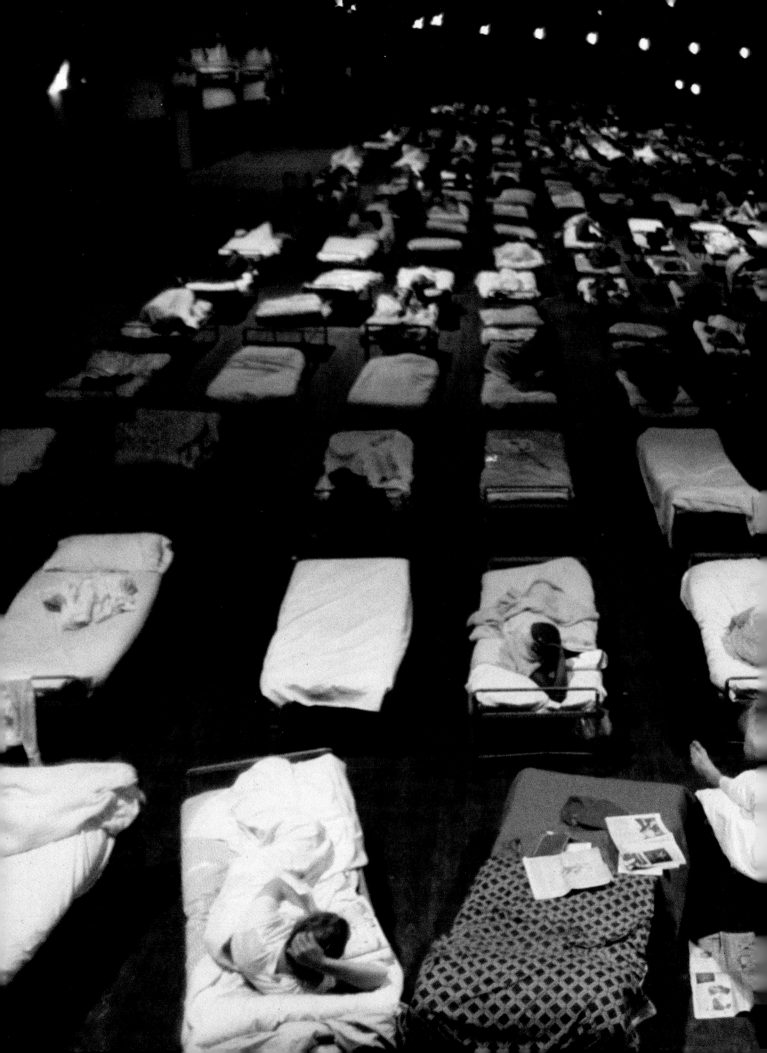

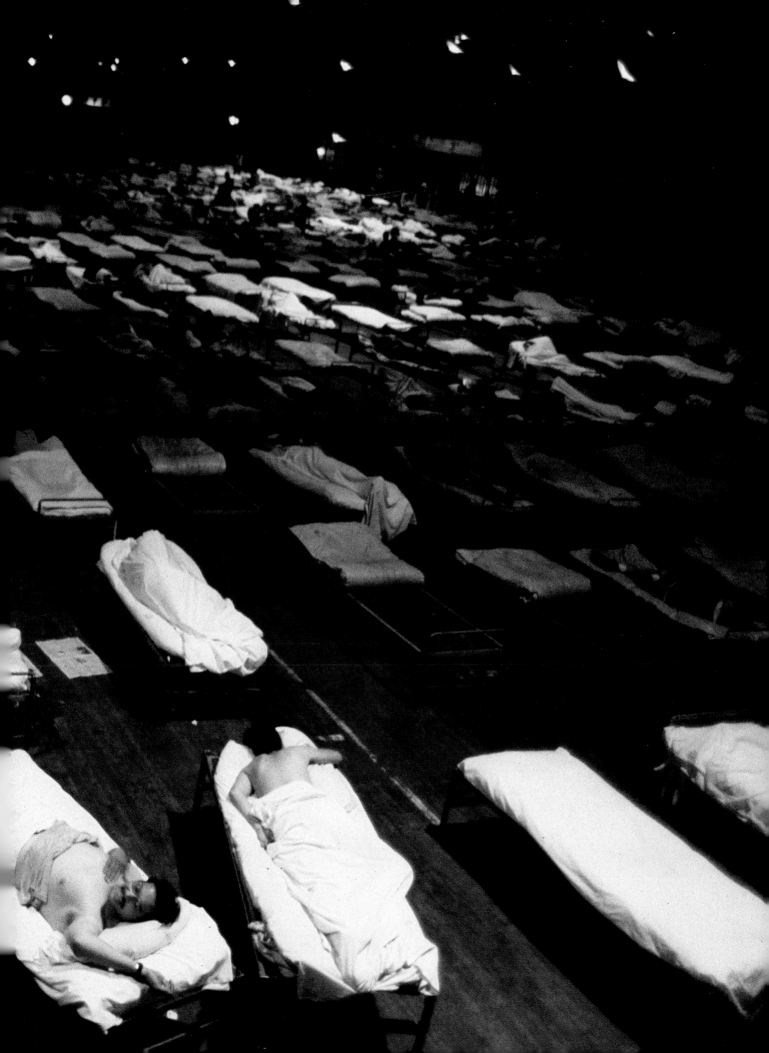

Pavement dweller, Bombay

Children in the City of the Dead, Cairo

Family living in a garbage dump, Cairo

Garbage pickers, Lagos

Homeless man, New York

MAKING ENDS MEET: PEOPLE AT WORK

Stockbrokers, Bombay

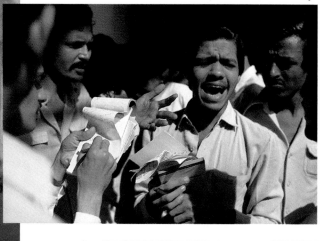

Goatherd, Cairo

Grocers, Moscow

Butcher, New York

Weavers, Shanghai

Sewer-repair crew, Mexico City

Counterman, Rome

Vegetable vendor, Cairo

Prostitutes, Bombay

Movie actor, Bombay

Market women, Lagos

Construction worker,
Mexico City

Fishmongers,
Tokyo

Garment workers,
New York

Factory worker, Moscow

Doctors, Shanghai

City council members, Lagos

Cop, New York

Looking up, Tokyo

Chowpatty strollers, Bombay

Haze on the Nile, Cairo

VIEWS OF THE CITY

*Shopping street,
Rome*

City Hall, Mexico City

Looking up, New York

Downtown skyline, Lagos

Fireworks over the Kremlin, Moscow

Dawn on the Suzhou, Shanghai

Tokyo

Moscow

THE AGING CITY

New York

Rome

Mexico City

Shanghai

THE CYCLE ENDS . . .

New York

Shanghai

Cairo

Lagos

Bombay

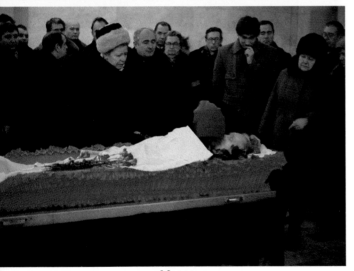

Moscow

Rome

Tokyo

. . . AND BEGINS AGAIN

Mexico City

"There are those who maintain that the future of the city
may well determine the future of the world. But whether
it does or it does not, it is already evident that when
we enter the new urban world in the next few years, we
will find ourselves in largely unexplored territory,
knowing more about the distant planets of outer space
than about the exploding cities of our own planet Earth. . . .
With no letup in sight, by the time the twenty-first
century passes its first quarter, the cities of the
Third World will be the overcrowded, congested home
of nearly four billion people, the poor, the homeless,
the pavement dwellers, the slum- and shantytown-confined,
the inadvertent, accidental pioneers of the new urban world."

Lagos' explosion has made it the fastest-growing city in Africa . . .

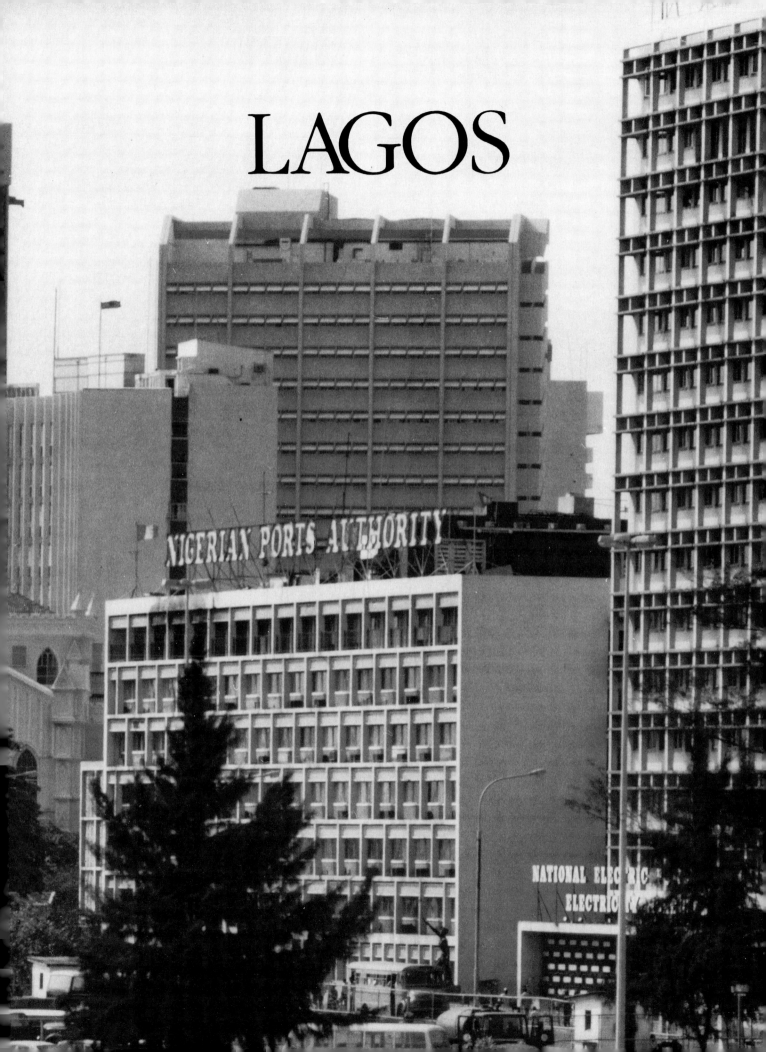

LAGOS

. . . struggling to catch up with itself and the needs of its people

Lagos' explosion has left it fighting two critical battles, and no one is quite sure how either one will turn out. The first is its struggle to catch up with itself, a task made all the more difficult because it keeps losing ground; and second, to counter its reputation as "one of the worst cities in the world," a lawless frontier town in conflict with itself.

As late as 1960, Lagos was a small metropolis of less than half a million people. Now, with twelve times that number, it is the most populous city in the most populous country in Africa.

Teeming with more than six million people, Lagos looks as if all the classic symptoms and problems of the urban explosion had come together in one place. The dilemma in which it finds itself had its beginnings early in the 1960s, when oil was discovered far away under the Niger delta in what for a time became Biafra and the battleground of a bitter and bloody civil war in which millions died.

A downtown garbage dump

Many migrants live in tin-roof shacks . . .

When the Lagos government won the war—and the revenue that went with the oil—it touched off a mass migration that made it appear as if the entire countryside were pouring into the city to share in its newfound wealth. But the bubble has long since burst and the people of Lagos now find themselves trapped in the middle of Nigeria's growing economic problems. They have one of two choices: either go back to the land, as some are doing, or stay put, which is the choice of most. And those who remain are being joined every day by hundreds of new arrivals who still come searching for an elusive future in the city.

Compounding all this for the Nigerians is the often harsh view of an outside world that sees Lagos as "a city out of control," as one account has put it, and "a byword for sweaty, ugly, greedy unpleasantness," according to another. Such opinions stir deep resentment and anger in Lagos, and it is not unknown for an unsuspecting visitor to be shouted at in the street and held personally accountable for every critical comment in the Western press. But there is also a quiet recognition by many that the city does, indeed, have symptoms of a serious malaise that must be treated.

The city's early occupiers left behind a heritage that has done much to shape today's climate. Certainly, it did not help prepare Lagos for its role as a modern giant supercity.

Made up of a cluster of small islands off the West African gold coast, Lagos was used by the Portuguese as a safe harbor for their flourishing seventeenth-century slave trade. A lagoon at the center provided the Portuguese name for one of the islands, and ultimately for the city that was to become the capital of Nigeria when the British literally created the country at the turn of the twentieth century.

. . . waiting for new housing in the new century

Unlike the rest of Africa, Nigeria has a long tradition of urbanization; but even that did not prepare Lagos for the human wave that swept into it once the tragic war with Biafra ended. They came not only from all over Nigeria, but from adjoining countries as well. Housing was overwhelmed, sewers were overloaded, power and water drained, roads and transport clogged. Even wealthy sections, once the preserve of high-living colonial administrators and international businessmen, were suddenly overrun. Lagos was a boom town with a vengeance. With crime and violence on the rise, it became known as a rough-and-tumble frontier city where visitors and residents alike were warned to keep off the streets at night—and, often as not, during the day, too.

But in a country that had so little, that was not enough to keep the migrants away from a city that had so much: Lagos is the capital of Nigeria and the capital of the state of Lagos, the country's largest port, its main industrial center and its most important commercial cross-

"Illegal" housing holds millions of squatters and refugees . . .

. . . from the African countryside

roads. It is, in addition, the seat of a giant federal bureaucracy, including some 20 state governments; headquarters of the military government that runs the country, as well as the headquarters of the military general staff and garrison; the headquarters also of the oil and other nationalized industries; and the base of operations for all the companies—Nigerian and international—that do business with the government and its many branches and agencies. All told, Lagos is the centerpiece of Nigeria's economic and political life, as much a magnet to the wealthy businessmen of stylish Victoria Island as it is to the poor market women of shabby Ajugenle.

From an original settlement of 1.5 square miles on Lagos Island, the city has grown into a metropolitan area of some 102 square miles, spreading out over the other islands in the lagoon and onto the mainland itself. Much of Lagos is built on wetland, and while that has been a major problem throughout its history, it is only one of many more than have grown along with the city itself.

In fact, Lagos officials are candid in saying their city today is a classic case history of haphazard development, that it lacks a planned, functioning infrastructure, and that city services are, to say the least, grossly inadequate. None of this, however, has been enough to stop even more growth; nor is that growth expected to stop before it covers some 1500 square miles. At that point, Lagos will be more than a city or metropolitan area. It will be the hub of what one of its many master plans anticipates will have become a vast metropolitan region made up of many urban centers.

For now, the migration that brought in as many as a thousand people a day has slowed, and there has even been a small turnaround. With housing being so difficult to come by, the job market long having passed its peak, and an increase in prices for once depressed farm goods in the rural areas, some young people have picked themselves up and headed back to the land. But the number is relatively small—one report put it at half a million—and Lagos still attracts newcomers at a rate double the overall national population growth rate.

Thus far millions of refugees have crowded into the city's wetlands and swamps and onto lonely sand ridges, squatting wherever they can find a dry spot on public or private land. Some live in makeshift housing of their own, others in city projects built so quickly that much of it is already beginning to deteriorate, some of it even sinking in the swamp. From time to time, not unlike Bombay, police raze the illegal housing, and a few days later most of it is back up again. The housing shortage is so acute that government agencies themselves frequently make use of an illegal building, "a sure way," according to one official, "to find out it's there!"

Whether it is in the wetlands or on Victoria Island—or in any other part of the city—the drive to get rich is inescapable. It is what served to spur the initial migration to Lagos and, difficult as things are there today, that drive remains, visible in a marketplace atmosphere that is a vital part of the city's mystique. Some say it now *is* the city, symbolizing the extent to which the rural way of life has become the prevailing way of life in Lagos. It manifests itself primarily in the daily struggle to make ends meet.

The high cost of living being what it is, those with regular jobs no less than those without must supplement their incomes just to get by. In the countryside, the most popular way is to be a "trader." In Lagos now, hundreds of thousands of people—some say a million may be closer to it—are doing just that, and the result is a city of noisy marketplaces swarming with traders.

With stereos and radios blaring at top volume and buyers and sellers negotiating in equally full voice, downtown streets are lined three and four deep with shops and stalls and carts selling every variety of goods. Traditional markets, some of them huge and cavernous airplane-hangar-type structures, are located in strategic areas, most run with an iron hand by street-smart market women, who have become a city institution as well as a potent political force.

Then, too, there is the "go-slow market" operated by a small army of retailers who buy and sell along routes of stalled and crawling traffic. And not to be overlooked are the private informal markets run by thousands of individuals (ranging from laborers to city officials) out of their homes and offices. If anything symbolizes Lagos today, it is this nonstop trading, day and night, in a city overwhelmed by the countryside and trying to use that influx to rebuild and revitalize itself.

One leading Nigerian urban planner says it will not be easy, that working in Lagos is like working in the dark without a flashlight. What makes a solution to its problems so hard to see is that they follow a pattern common to most other Third World cities: They are a microcosm of the larger problems of the country as a whole.

Traders plying a miscellany of wares . . .

Conceding that point (without quite saying so), the country's current development plan seeks to decentralize investment away from Lagos and thereby encourage industry and commerce to resettle in other parts of the country. In keeping with this aim, which is to remove the incentive that draws people to Lagos, the plan also calls for the removal of the federal capital itself to another city, Abuja, near the geographical center of Nigeria.

. . . spill over into sidewalks and streets

The market women of Lagos form an important social and political group

But even if this plan is ultimately carried out—and many question whether it will be—that alone will not do much to ease Lagos' growing pains before the end of the century. Nor will other measures being talked about, such as increasing the supply of low-cost housing, improving the transportation system, including a high-speed elevated metroline, and better environmental conditions. If anything, the fear

Children in the most populous city in the most populous country in Africa . . .

is that these steps will only make Lagos even more attractive than it already is to rural migrants, whose numbers are expected to grow along with Nigeria's overall population.

With nearly half of all Nigerians under fifteen years of age, and less than three percent sixty-five or older, the country's present-day population of 115 million—making it the eighth largest country in the world—is almost sure to pass 165 million by the year 2000, and 280 million by the year 2015. Then, 16 million people, more than two and a half times as many as today, are expected to be living in Lagos, an unsettling prospect for a city trying to contain its growth. Of even greater concern is that the majority—both in Lagos and in the country at large—will still be in the prime of their childbearing years.

. . . in which most people are still not in their child-bearing prime

". . . I want to help [as an architect] make Africa into a developed continent . . . and build a safer, less crowded Lagos. . . ."

"Our problems go back to the colonial period. . . . We inherited a system that is outdated and must now be modernized to serve our needs today. . . . Certainly, we do have problems, but remember, we are trying to do in a few years what has taken other cities a century and more. . . . We will make it . . . because [we] have what it takes to remake our image no less than our city itself. . . ."
—Sole Administrator Y. O. Basorum

Nigeria, with one-sixth of all of the continent's inhabitants, has recently initiated a voluntary family planning program described as "the most ambitious in Africa." The greatest impact has been in Lagos, where the birthrate is already lower than anywhere else in the country. However, this decrease has been more than offset by the continued arrival of newcomers from the rural areas, where the birthrate is soaring.

Lagos' explosion, therefore, is far from over. Fewer refugees are making the trek today compared to the height of the boom a few years ago, but no one can say for sure their numbers will not increase again. Until conditions in the rest of the country improve, not even the city's struggle to escape from the swamp in which history and geography have combined to leave it may be enough to keep hopeful newcomers out.

Tokyo has been virtually rebuilt from the ground up

TOKYO

In 1945, Tokyo was a city of smoking ruins and ashes. Today it is the second-largest city in the world and certainly one of the most modern and affluent.

Like Mexico City and all other exploding cities, Tokyo must cope with a cross-section of urban ills left behind in the wake of its remarkable growth. But any similarity ends there. Tokyo is a wealthy city in a wealthy country.

In the decade of the 1970s, Tokyo supplanted New York as the world's largest city until Mexico City, in turn, overtook it early in 1986

(though some demographers, citing the fuzzy definition of the city's metropolitan borders, say Tokyo is still the largest). The capital in every sense of the word of Japan's national and international life, Tokyo has become a hard-driving "corporate town," as well as the country's springboard for nearly everything of importance that goes on in Japan. The city never seems to slow down, pulsating with activity and throbbing with life and energy day and night. But in spite of all the nonstop crowds and equally nonstop activities, Tokyo has contained its explosion.

The people of Tokyo: a wealthy city . . .

. . . in a wealthy country

True, the city's population is still going up, but at a steadily declining rate. With more than 17 million people packed into the Tokyo-Yokohama complex of the Kanto Plain, the population of the Greater Tokyo area is expected to peak at 17.2 million by 1990, and then start to ebb for the first time since World War II. This decline is consistent with a population that is getting older all the time, and it now appears almost inevitable that Tokyo will mark the year 2000 as one of the new century's first cities of the aged.

Not much of Tokyo was left standing after the massive air raids of 1945. Indeed, what with its long history of earthquakes and fires, there is little of anything that is still standing from the time the city emerged as the capital of Japan in 1868 (when it was given its present name, meaning, appropriately enough, Eastern Capital). Even less survives from the centuries before then, when it was an obscure fishing village known as Edo.

Tokyo is not a beautiful city in the conventional sense of the word. The greater part of it is made up of a series of onetime villages huddled together to form the larger city, a sprawling, congested conurbation covering nearly a thousand square miles. Put together, it is a jumble of shabby old and sparkling new residential neighbor-hoods, industrial areas, business and shopping districts, amusement centers, and shrines and temples all thrown together in no discernible pattern.

The Imperial palace grounds aside, there is precious little green space—indeed any open space—in the architectural clutter that is Tokyo today: rickety wooden buildings and bathhouses of uncertain age, row after row of uniformly designed stone-and-brick high rises, towering steel-and-glass skyscrapers, nameless twisting roads and streets and a myriad of identical avenues and boulevards, all choked with traffic. In essence, Tokyo is largely a product of some forty years of intensive, almost frenzied, building and growth; and with the old, the new, and the in-between crushed together side by side, intermin-gling and overlapping, it is hard to tell where one ends and the other begins.

Sunday on the Ginza—no traffic, many people

Tokyo: a city nearly destroyed in the war . . .

Frequent tremors are a constant reminder of earthquakes. And while this has resulted in construction codes and practices to make buildings fireproof and shockproof, it has not interfered with the city's miraculous rebirth since the war, not with the explosion that tripled its population in two decades: from 3 million in 1945 to 10 million plus in 1965. By 1980, the metropolitan area alone was overflowing with 11.1 million people, and Tokyo had surpassed New York as the largest city in the world; the dubious title is assumed along with the housing shortages, the inner-city congestion and blight, the traffic tie-ups, the pollution, and the other classic scars of explosion. In contrast to most other wealthy cities and, of course, those in the Third World, not in evidence on Tokyo streets are any visible signs of poverty.

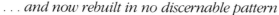

. . . and now rebuilt in no discernable pattern

Non-stop traffic . . . non-stop crowds (overleaf)

Other problems, however, are much in evidence, but so, too, is an effort to overcome them. Typical is the strict enforcement of anti-pollution laws that gradually are dissipating what had become a chronic photo-chemical smog. Alerts still occur, but the worst seems over, and blue skies and clear nights are not uncommon again.

Traffic is still bad. A ten- or fifteen-minute drive in the middle of the night may take an hour or two and even longer at midday. Mass transit is one of the best and also just about one of the most congested anywhere (riding in the subway is a test that sorely tries—and often overcomes—even vaunted Japanese courtesy).

My Town Tokyo: "returning to Tokyo its heart," where young people . . .

Housing remains in short supply, especially in the inner parts of the city, where real estate prices and rentals are among the highest in the world. One result is that many young Japanese choose to live in the outskirts, with a two-to-three-hour daily commute a normal part of their routine (which they accept stoically, if not happily).

In looking to the future, Tokyo has undertaken an ambitious $100 billion urban-revival program, popularly known by its advertising slogan title, "My Town Tokyo." The program's professed aim is to create what it calls a twenty-first-century "multinucleus city," in which various activities—industrial, business, residential, governmental, shopping, and cultural—will be more evenly distributed throughout the various neighborhoods of the metropolitan area.

The essence of the plan is decentralization (the goal of virtually every major city in the world) through the creation of nine self-contained subcenters, each with high-rise apartment houses, office buildings, shopping centers, recreation facilities, and whatever else would either eliminate or cut commuting time to the bone. Part of the plan also envisages linking the subcenters with both suburban and inner-city rail lines. And in all, the concept is a grand one, to say the least.

. . . "will shoulder the future . . . and the elderly live happily"

Some, in fact, call the plan "grandiose," and question if it will get off the drawing board in its entirety. Whether it does or not, many heavy industries and polluting factories have already moved from the city center to outlying areas. And many large corporate headquarters offices, including the municipal government itself, are also shifting from old, overcrowded districts to newer, smarter sections. The only trouble is the crowds follow the moves.

ここにコタツをおいたのは
ここの作品がつまらない
ということもうなみにみる
んじゃないかと思った
からだけど

肩書きを持つたのが大けれ
作家活動にはやん、よ

"My generation must . . . help those who need it in Africa . . . [and] wherever life is hard. . . ."

"I . . . have an earnest desire to return to Tokyo its 'heart' . . . the warmth of human feeling. . . . My vision is of a city [in which] people are united by a deep feeling of community and mutual assistance . . . the elderly and the disabled can live happily in peace and security, and the young people, who will shoulder the future [of Tokyo], can grow up to [lead] healthy and happy lives . . . a city [we are] proud to call home."

—Governor Shunichi Suzuki

Meanwhile, the city is beginning to turn its attention to the growing numbers of its elderly, building more health and welfare facilities and expanding a variety of social services for them. The fact is that the percentage of the aged is going up faster in Japan than in any of the other industrialized countries.

From 12.5 million, or 10.3 percent, in 1985, the number of people 65 or older in Japan will go up to 21.3 million, or 16.3 percent, by the year 2000; and by 2025, it will reach 31.5 million, or 23.4 percent. And with 10 percent of the country's total population, Tokyo may well be the largest "aging city" of the twenty-first century. And here its growth as a corporate and service city may stand Tokyo in good stead. With industries that will be largely computerized and automated, the city will have a reservoir of retirees to call on for jobs in which age will be less of a factor.

The full impact of its aging population will not be known for some time, but with an annual growth rate of only .7 percent nationwide, Tokyo's population, old and young together, will be declining by the end of the century. Nonetheless, the city is searching for new and innovative ways to end a crowding that in the year 2000 will be worse—if that is possible—than it is today.

Available land is already virtually nonexistent, and if and when a parcel does come on the market, the demand has pushed prices up to a point where even graveyard plots are hard to come by, and even harder to afford in land-hungry Tokyo. There is some talk now of developing the city underground, and a parliamentary group is looking into the possibility of relocating the capital, or at least some of its functions, as one way of freeing up land and bringing prices down.

But no one really looks to the removal of the capital as a likely measure, at least not in the foreseeable future. One direction in which Tokyo actually is looking is out to sea. There, in Tokyo Bay, it is now building an artificial island. And while that alone will not solve the city's crying need for more space, it will provide just a little more elbow room, even if only temporarily, for the move into the twenty-first century.

Reay Road . . . at the heart of Bombay's dilemma

BOMBAY

More than nine million people live in the metropolitan region of Bombay, half of them in the largest slum in Asia, a vast and still spreading shantytown called Dharavia. Another half a million are homeless squatters, or "pavement dwellers," in the heart of the city. And they are at the heart, too, of an agonizing dilemma.

This dilemma stems from Bombay's efforts to decongest itself by ousting the pavement dwellers from streets they had taken over as their own for nearly every aspect of living, no matter how personal or

private. Some call the action a legal paradox ("How can you dispossess the dispossessed?" they ask) and for years the issue has been fought out both in the courts and on the streets.

No satisfactory answer has yet been forthcoming. On and off there is talk of a barrier of sorts to keep new migrants out; but whatever the ultimate outcome, it is bound to be remembered as one of the most complex of the many difficult and troubling issues encountered by an exploding city anywhere in the world.

Living on the pavement: "How can you dispossess the dispossessed?"

Bombay's action, which became known as "the eviction of the homeless," had been prompted by a density that in some sections exceeds 200,000 persons per square mile. Even those who opposed the move agreed that something had to be done.

One leading critic says Bombay looks as if it had gone insane. "How long," asks another, "before the neglect, the piles of debris, the stinking garbage take their toll?"

But the refugees come anyway. To them, Bombay still has the glamour associated with a not too distant past, when it was India's own version of El Dorado. Even now, with life a daily struggle for most, it remains a place of extraordinary vitality. The city where Gandhi lived—his home is now a memorial—Bombay is the country's wealthiest and most important industrial and commercial center, its financial capital, its largest and busiest port, and, not least, its movie capital—all factors that make it a natural magnet for India's jobless millions.

Action on a Bombay movie set

Bombay's rich past is part of its allure

Refugee family, newly arriving from the country

The result is that Bombay's annual growth rate is double that of the rest of India, half of it coming from a continuing stream of refugees—300 to 400 families a day—from every part of the country. Now, with a population of 9.2 million people, Bombay may well be "groaning under the weight" of more than 16 million at the turn of the century, with most of the newcomers winding up in Dharavia or on the pavement. The projection for the year 2000, incidentally, is just about the same in Bombay as it is in Calcutta, a city whose name has become almost synonymous with the problems of the homeless. Yet the situation in Bombay is not much different, and in some ways it may even be worse.

The opulent Taj Mahal hotel

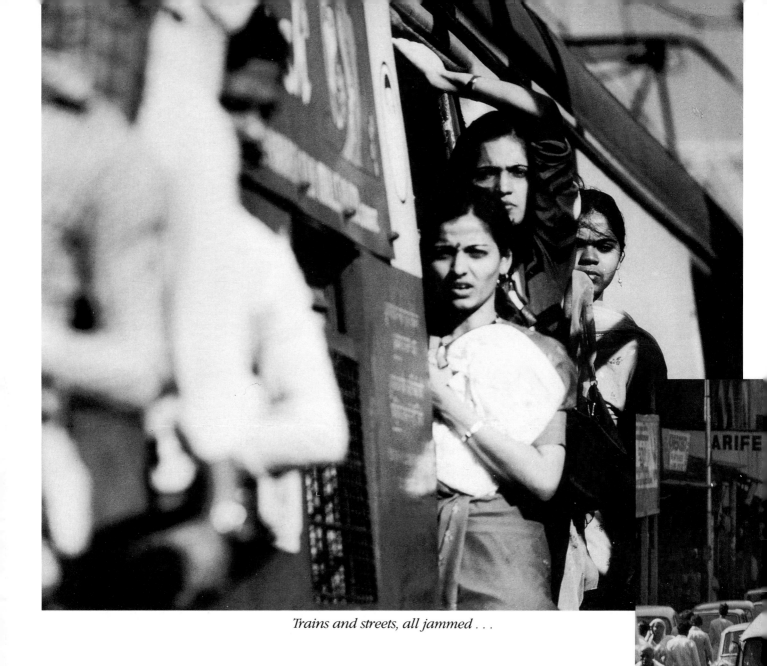

Trains and streets, all jammed . . .

The migrants aside, many of Bombay's problems stem from geography. Bombay is an island. On a map, it resembles an inverted triangle, its apex resting in the waters of the Arabian Sea off western Central India. Here, in 1668, the British East India Company turned a small fishing village made up of seven insignificant islands into a major link on the shipping route between Suez and Singapore. In the early 1930s, Bombay still had a population under a million; then, with the war and its aftermath, it jumped to three million in just one generation, and the explosion that in the next three decades transformed it into an "urban octopus" was underway.

Blocked by the sea at its apex, the triangular city could grow in one direction only, and its base is now on the mainland some twenty-six miles north of where it started. At no point, however, is the triangle more than one and a half miles wide, giving it the appearance, as one prominent Bombay architect aptly put it, of a taut, stretched-out rubber band about to snap.

142

Yet everyone wants to be in the apex. It is the site of the old port area developed by the British; it is also the brain center and heart of Bombay, the site of its business and financial centers, entertainment and cultural activities, hotels, restaurants, train and bus depots. And it is also the home of a huge government complex, both for the city itself and for the state of Maharashtra, of which Bombay is the capital.

The apex is where many of the wealthy live, and where, at times (or so it seems), all of Bombay—rich and poor—comes to stroll along the Chowpatty waterfront or sit on the embankment in the evenings, looking out at the Queen's Necklace, the blinking harbor lights that follow the curve of the original village's natural breakwater.

. . . with morning commuters

With so much activity going on in the old port area, more than 72 percent of all the jobs in Bombay are concentrated there. So, beginning hours before dawn, an unending line of overfilled trains, buses, cars, bicycles, and horse-drawn carts all pour down the narrow length of the triangle, bringing commuters to work in the concrete high-rise jungle of Nariman Point and Cuffe Parade. One-way commuting times of two to three hours and more are not unusual, and neither are the interminable traffic jams. Nor is the burning smog, a noxious blend of the exhaust from the city's 4.5 million vehicles, most of them old, and the pollutants discharged into the air by a heavy concentration of factories, most of them old, too, ranging from textile to cement.

The port area makes up 15 percent of the metropolitan region, and the critics contend that its continued development will ultimately strangle Bombay. City services already are badly strained, with the southern tip, the most desirable part of town, getting the lion's share. Garbage collection, sewage, public transport—the rest of the city must either make do with "leftover" amenities, or do without entirely. Broken water lines are everywhere, the pools they form becoming open-air bathhouses for the homeless, who have literally taken possession of the pavements.

A family in Dharavia, the biggest slum in Asia

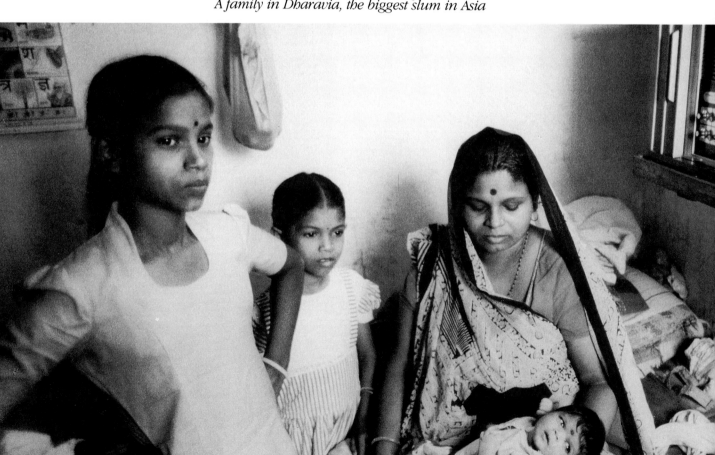

Many Bombay factories, like this textile mill, are antiquated

Some pavement dwellers have no set place, sleeping in the open, unfolding their bedding while traffic and pedestrians swirl around them. Others live in hovels propped up against the side of a building, a tree, a shrub, anything that will support a makeshift wall. From time to time police clear the streets, bulldoze the shacks, and return the

Three with no home at all

property to its private and public owners, including the city itself. Bloody battles have erupted on the streets, and the courts have struggled with the dilemma since the early 1980s. In the meanwhile, outsted from one street, the pavement dwellers pick up their meager possessions and move to another.

Aggravating the situation is a desperate shortage of affordable housing that is also safe. At least 40 percent of Bombay's housing is vacant because it is uninhabitable, while 15 percent of all people who do have housing live in some 20,000 buildings on the verge of collapse. Nearly a million people are on the waiting list for low-rent municipal housing, a number that continues to escalate as more and more migrants come to Bombay to stay.

The growth of Dharavia and the pavement-dweller population is a direct result of this housing shortage. By this time, Dharavia is a city within a city, with its own transport, schools, markets, clinics, and even playgrounds and theaters. It houses a large part of Bombay's work force, people who pay rent but cannot afford to pay the going rate in the city proper.

Pavement dwellers pay no rent—which is one of the inducements—but they, too, are an important part of the city's labor pool. In fact, in one 1985 survey of 6000 families, some 27,000 people whose homes were on the street, disclosed that 43 percent were wage earners, compared to 36 percent of the population as a whole. (But they earn far less than the minimum wage, which means they cannot afford even the rent they would have to pay for a slum in Dharavia.) Eyesore and all, if the pavement dwellers were to disappear without being replaced, the city's industries would be hard pressed without them; and this, Bombay planners say, provides another compelling reason to spread out the concentration of industry and services packed into the city's apex. Indeed, representatives of the homeless insist that until that happens, not even low-income housing and other inducements, such as giving them the land at nominal cost, will entice the squatters to leave the streets of the inner city and move to the outskirts of the metropolitan area.

Getting a reluctant business and industry to make the first move, all agree, is thus a prerequisite if Bombay Island, the heart of the city, is to be decongested and all of Bombay saved. An area known as New Bombay across the harbor from the old port has its supporters who believe that is where the city's future lies; and construction actually has been going on there for the past decade. (Some planners originally had hoped the migrants would settle there, but it didn't work out, although there have been signs of a possible turnaround.) And there is also considerable support for going north to the suburbs, where some industrial and residential construction has already started, but which for the most part is still in the planning stage.

SIR PHROZESHAH MEHTA GARDEN
— NOTICE —

1) ANY TYPE OF EXERCISES ARE NOT ALLOWED IN THE GARDEN
2) SLEEPING IN THE GARDEN IS NOT ALLOWED
3) DOGS ARE NOT ALLOWED WITHOUT A CHAIN
4) DRINKING OF LIQUOR IS NOT ALLOWED IN THE GARDEN
5) EATING ANY EATABLES IS NOT ALLOWED
6) DO NOT PLUCK THE FLOWERS
7) ANY TYPE OF PLAY SUCH ASFOOT BALL,
   CRICKET, FLYING KITE
8) PHOTHO GRAPHY WITH THE MOVIE CAMERA IS TOTALLY PROHIBITED
9) BAD DEEDS ARE PROHIBITED

BY ORDER

"Our school motto says it is better to light candles than curse the darkness . . . and that is what we must do in Bombay."

"Bombay's problems are there for everyone to see, they stare at you from every street corner. . . . [They are] man-made problems and we must come up with man-made solutions . . . so that we have a clean city, a city in which we can walk on the streets. . . . We are trying to jump from the eighteenth to the twentieth century in one leap. . . ."

—Mayor Shri Chagan Bhujbal

Whatever and wherever its future, the reality is that Bombay has a difficult time ahead of it. India's overall population today stands at 817 million, with one-quarter of it living in slums and shantytowns and on the pavement. The Indian government is trying to promote the wider use of voluntary family planning and thereby reduce the population growth rate from 3.3 percent to 1.1 percent by the end of the century; but even if it succeeds, the country's population is still expected to top one billion in the year 2000 and eventually pass China as the most populous nation in the world. Bombay's schools and health clinics are taking an active role in advancing the government's effort, and one survey has it that at least half the married women in the city already practice some form of birth control. But tradition dies hard.

Meanwhile, what happens in Bombay in the next few years—both the extent to which its population growth rate is lowered and what it actually does to make itself smaller and more manageable—will be a barometer for the rest of the country. The way some see it, Bombay's choices are limited: It can wind up the century either as a warning to other cites or as "a successful experiment" in saving itself.

The tomb of Lenin outside the Kremlin walls: a waiting line is always there

MOSCOW

The towers of the Kremlin

In that same time, too, Moscow has just about doubled its size. But this growth only partially reflects the city's special appeal in a country that considers it not just its capital, but literally its heart. Moscow's unique status in the Soviet Union is grounded in history and emotion and makes for a recurring theme in Russian literature. "Moscow . . ." Aleksander Pushkin wrote, "what thoughts to each true-hearted Russian come flooding at that word. . . ." And indeed, if all the bars were down, the city would be flooded with a population many times more than the 8.7 million people who already live there.

This has not happened because Moscow's growth—as all growth in the Soviet Union, urban or rural—is carefully monitored and regulated by the government to an extent unknown in Mexico City or Cairo or Bombay. Today, in fact, no more than 60,000 people a year may move to the Soviet capital from elsewhere in the country—and then only if they are assured of a job there in advance or are admitted to one of Moscow's many schools, or get married to a Muscovite who has an apartment.

Weekend horse-racing at the "Hippodrom"

New "housing estates" are built with prefabricated parts

The emotional reasons aside, Moscow's drawing power is broadly based and powerful. In 1919, Lenin called for it to be a model city for the entire country, and today as the political capital of one of the world's great superpowers, it is also the ideological, administrative, economic, and cultural capital of the entire Soviet system. Very little of any consequence happens without some Moscow involvement.

Standing on the banks of the Moskva River (and on the site of an Iron Age settlement), the city is situated at the hub of the country's busiest crossroads connecting its main industrial regions. A major manufacturing center in its own right, with more than 1600 factories and other industrial enterprises, Moscow brings together a large government bureaucracy, including at least one-quarter of all the country's research scientists. It is the campus for some 76 institutions of higher learning with an academic population of more than 650,000, and many of the country's and the world's most famed concert halls, ballet companies, and theaters are also at home there.

Moscow's 650,000 students and professors are a vital part of the city

Father and son in one of Moscow's parks

The pre-fab units in place: the master plan hopes to give every family an apartment by the year 2000

With all its many attractions, however, the careful control being exerted over its growth makes Moscow the very antithesis of an exploding city. Every aspect of its development is meticulously laid out in a master plan that charts the city's future right through to the end of the first decade of the twenty-first century, when its population is expected to reach 10.6 million. Right now Moscow could not house that many people; it is having difficulties housing its present population, and this is one of the prime reasons given for limiting the number of people who may move there today.

Actually, Moscow's chronic apartment shortage is nothing new. It goes back to the days before the Russian Revolution in 1917, when it became the capital. Although the rebuilding of the city since the end of World War II has included some 90 percent of all its housing, even

Annual Leningrad-Moscow rally

that has not been enough to eliminate the need for communal apartments shared by two or more families.

Today, 20 percent of all Muscovites still live in such apartments, and it is a source of considerable grumbling; few priorities in the master plan rate higher than the one that aims to end the shortage by the year 2000.

For all the changes in its physical exterior, Moscow remains a city long on history and tradition, and its classic image is still a strong one: the architectural grandeur of a centuries-old Kremlin with its tent-roofed towers and silver palaces, the grand medieval churches and cathedrals capped by golden domes and multicolored cupolas, the fifteenth-century marketplace—now Red Square—with the tomb of Lenin off to one side. This is the picture-postcard image Moscow projects. But it is incomplete.

Going downtown to eat ice cream—no matter what the temperature

A walk through its complex tangle of old cobblestone streets and broad new avenues also shows a Moscow with a modern skyline steadily pushing upward. At one time, apartment houses were limited to four and five stories; now seventeen and twenty stories are commonplace. Sleek new hotels and office buildings rise higher still, at times towering over a tiny church, its size and age an abrupt reminder of the city's changing face.

And as the city pushes upward, it is also expanding outward and now covers two and a half times more ground—some 600 square miles—than it did at the end of the war in 1945. Under the master plan, the expectation is that it will continue to push outward past an encircling ring highway that cuts its way through the woods surrounding Moscow. Then, early in the next century, the planners say, work will start on three satellite cities complete with industries and housing designed to help ease pressure on the inner city.

Moscow is rapidly becoming a city "of new houses and old people"

A large-scale decentralization program has already started, with the city divided into several zones made up of massive self-contained housing "estates," most of the buildings put together from prefabricated parts. These estates house 100,000 to 300,000 people and are virtually identical minitowns, almost small cities, each with its own schools, shopping centers, health complexes, cultural activities, entertainment facilities, and even helicopter pads. The aim in building them on the outskirts is to cut back on traffic and congestion—both people and cars—to and from the inner city (although what passes for congestion in Moscow would be a welcome relief in Bombay or Cairo).

But not all Muscovites are happy about the idea of decentralization. The outskirts, no matter how attractive, are no match for the inner city's appeal. Red Square, the Arbat, Gorky Street, Kalinin Avenue, the museums, the opera, the Bolshoi, the stores, or just walking—the reason is secondary to the Muscovites' urge to "go downtown." Not even the most frigid days of the year deter them. The temperature may be subzero, snow falling, breath vaporizing, but streets and boulevards are crowded with strollers eating ice cream; meanwhile, long queues wait patiently for hours to enter a museum to see a new exhibit, or to shop in a store that has received a new shipment. In Moscow no less than in Mexico City or New York, going downtown is an ingrained habit, hard to break. And everyone agrees it will not be easy to convince those who now live in the inner city (where getting an apartment, even one to share, is considered akin to a miracle) to pick up and move to the outskirts, even if the reward is an end to sharing and a prized flat all their own.

"... I want to be an engineer and work for the improvement of the atmosphere ... and for peace ... [which is] the world's biggest problem. ..."

"We are proud of our city. ... We have our problems, of course, but we are working hard to resolve them. ... We share a commitment to urban living ... and to the advancement [of Moscow's] harmonious development. ... We are making progress in improving both the living and working conditions of all Muscovites. ... My wishes for the new century are for everyone to have their own apartment ... to have more green space ... better mass transit ... but above all, my wish for the year 2000 is to have peaceful skies over Moscow. ..."

—Chairman of the Moscow City Council Valery Timoleyevich Saikin

The controls in effect in Moscow have gone a long way in preventing the growth of any serious urban decay or crime; nor are there any homeless wandering the streets. But Moscow does have its share of other urban problems common to most other cities today. Beginning with its housing shortage, these are not all that different from what is being encountered elsewhere: insufficient mass transit (paradoxically, the subway system is one of the best anywhere), traffic tie-ups, environmental hazards and pollution, a need for more green space and recreational facilities—all matters of concern for city dwellers the world over. And not unlike city officials elsewhere, the members of the Moscow City Council worry about where they will find the money to keep their city running smoothly.

Meanwhile, getting more and more attention these days is the subtle change taking place in the age structure of the city's population, a situation again very similar to what is happening in Tokyo and Shanghai, in New York and Rome and other major cities.

Moscow's birthrate is going down—it is now down to 1.43 percent, and in all likelihood will be lower still in the year 2000—but the number of its pensioners, the catch-all word for everyone past sixty-five and retired, is going up. Now nearing the two million mark, pensioners will total one-quarter of the city's overall population by the end of the century. Industries in Moscow are already beginning to feel the effect in the labor pool, one that Moscow planners think will continue, at least until the apartment shortage ends. And by then "we may well be a city," one pensioner quips, "of new houses and old people."

But it is unlikely the situation will ever really reach that point, not if the apartment shortages eases, as the master plan calls for, and the economy expands, as the government hopes. Then more people will be permitted to move into Moscow, and no one thinks it will be hard to recruit them.

Summer day, Central Park

NEW YORK

To walk in Central Park on a sunny Sunday afternoon is to join in a parade of people from virtually every country in the world, their faces a constantly revolving kaleidoscope of the rich ethnic and racial mix that makes New York City the most heterogeneous of any great city today or in history.

The variety of New York's population has perhaps always been its single most striking feature. And while this diversity is not lessening—if anything, the mix is getting richer—there are profound changes taking place in it that have far-reaching implications for the city in the new century.

New York is the most heterogeneous city in the world today . . .

• Blacks, Hispanics, and Asians now outnumber whites, a momentous shift in the status quo that evolved in less than a generation. As late as 1980, although the change was already evident, the majority was still white. By the year 2000, nonwhites and Hispanics will account for 60 percent of the population.

• A disproportionate number of the darker faces one sees are also the faces of the poor and homeless. Today, one in four New Yorkers lives in poverty, two-thirds of the total women and children. By the year 2000, with 40 percent of all of its children among the poor today, the city may well have a permanent poverty population, or underclass, of as much as 20 to 25 percent of its overall population.

. . . the variety of its population is its single most striking feature

• The people of New York are getting older, with nearly one in five now past the age of sixty, some 350,000 of them past the age of seventy-five. By the year 2000, the ratio will be higher still, especially the number of "old old" past eighty-five, and New York will then be another of the twenty-first century's cities of the aged.

Today, New York City is coping with a series of daunting economic and social problems that run through the entire fabric of its urban structure. The dynamic growth that earlier in the century made it the world's largest city—and one of the wealthiest—has slowed. Among other things, a good part of what had been a flourishing and highly profitable manufacturing industry either dried up or went elsewhere (where costs were less), contributing to the city's loss at the height of it all of 600,000 jobs.

One in five New Yorkers . . .

. . . is now past the age of sixty

The Williamsburg Bridge, closed for repairs

Wall Street

But for all the scars left by a near brush with bankruptcy in the 1970s, New York City in the past few years has made what everyone agrees is a remarkable turnaround. A special Mayor's Commission on the Year 2000 (set up to help plan the city's future in the new century) found that while the city now faces serious competition from other parts of the United States and the world, by the turn of the century it should again be "the unrivaled world city," a dynamic international capital and symbol of America itself, gateway to its economy and "the center of creativity in just about every field. . . ."

The jagged, dramatic skyline that has become the city's trademark straddles a crowded global crossroads of business, finance, communication, science, technology, education, culture, and the arts. Testing ground for the new and headquarters for countless endeavors, New York is the composite of what Lewis Mumford must have had in mind when he likened big cities to museums where "every variety of human functions, every technological process, every mode of architecture and planning can be found somewhere within its crowded area. . . ."

Also to be found are the extremes that cut through a cross-section of the city: great wealth and great poverty, luxury high rises and bombed-out slum tenements, upwardly mobile yuppie enclaves and stagnating inner-city ghettos, deserted patches that look as if the city forgot they existed, and glossy new stretches that stand on the very threshold of the twenty-first century.

As the core of a sprawling metropolitan area, New York City spills over parts of three states, with a spit of it jutting a hundred miles or so out into the Atlantic Ocean. That view covers 20,663 square miles and holds a regional population of 19.6 million people.

Within the confines of its city lines, New York's size shrinks to 520 square miles, with a population of 7.2 million people living in five relatively small boroughs situated at the mouth of New York Harbor. That was where the city had its seventeenth-century beginnings—first as a Dutch and then as a British colonial outpost—on the southern tip of Manhattan Island.

A "burned out" tenement on upper Park Avenue

One of the biggest and busiest ports—air and sea—in the world, New York over the years has seen an almost unending stream of immigrants and refugees literally pour into the great melting pot that it became. Not even two global conflicts slowed down a flow that goes on today with one exception: The mostly white European influx that helped shape the city in the late-eighteenth and early-nineteenth centuries has now given way to a new wave from the Caribbean, Latin America, and Southeast Asia.

As it is, the city's foreign-born population—one in every four New Yorkers—is at a seventy-five-year high, and this does not include half a million or so "hidden" New Yorkers, or illegal aliens without immigration permits. And in the remaining years of the century, between 750,000 and 1,250,000 more new immigrants—most of them part of the wave from the Caribbean, Latin America, and Asia—are expected to add their numbers to the melting pot, further increasing the diversity of people, ethnic neighborhoods, and cultural institutions that are the heart of New York.

Faces of "the melting pot" (see overleaf)

Poverty in the midst of wealth: the homeless.

But the same diversity that distinguishes it is also the source of one of New York's biggest and most painful problems. In the city's mix, blacks are the largest single group. Hispanics, mainly Puerto Ricans, are next. And it is these two groups that are hit by poverty harder than any other. In a city in which the majority of the population is "making it," they—blacks and Hispanics—remain largely poor.

In fact, the Commission on the Year 2000 found that the number of blacks and Hispanics affected by poverty is so disproportionate that it is inextricably linked to the parallel problem of race relations in the city. A wide body of opinion goes beyond that, holding it is the racial issue itself that makes for the city's single most important problem; but whichever tops the list, race or poverty, few disagree that to combat one means combating the other as well "if New York is to develop to its full potential. . . ."

A sign of poverty particularly hard to miss because it is so incongruous in the midst of wealth is the growing number of homeless people walking the streets, carrying their possessions in a shopping bag or piled up in a pushcart. The like of it has not been seen in

Although their numbers are relatively small compared to Bombay and Lagos . . .

New York since the days of the Great Depression more than half a century ago; now the number living on the streets or in various city shelters is well up in the thousands. If it continues to grow, as seems likely, it is almost sure to surpass that of the 1930s. The total, of course, is minuscule compared to the millions of homeless in the Third World, but already parts of the city are being referred to as "Calcutta, U.S.A."

Adding to the human problems coming to a head in the closing years of the century are a troublingly high crime rate compounded by drugs, a health-care system strained by the AIDS epidemic, and an educational system suffering from an excessive dropout rate that helps perpetuate black and Hispanic poverty.

there are more homeless today than at any time since the Depression

Cannibalized car—a common sight

Subway graffiti: a New York signature

And then there is the city's infrastructure, the physical problems that cannot be put off any longer: a serious housing shortage that has been called New York's Achilles heel, gridlock traffic that paralyzes the city's busiest sections, a mass-transportation system that is seriously overcrowded and often dangerous, decaying bridges that threaten to tumble into the rivers they span, and more. All this is seen as the price the city is paying for having grown too fast, too dense, and too large, winding up with what today is a physical plant—parks, subways, bridges, buildings—that "look more like ancient ruins than the functioning components of a great city."

Few New Yorkers take issue with that appraisal. What softens it is the recovery, in part, at least, from what has been called "one of the most shattering experiences in its history—its economic decline and fiscal crisis. . . ." While far from being out of the fiscal woods, there is wide consensus that the extent of the city's recovery would not have been dreamed possible only a decade ago.

192

New York's garbage: disposing of it is one of the major problems facing the city

New York's yesterday . . .

Indeed, starting in the mid-1980s, New York's economy has seen the largest sustained job growth since mid-century, and the Commission on the Year 2000 optimistically hopes—although no one will guarantee it—that the city's employment rate in the year 2000 will be as high as it was in 1969, which has been singled out as a peak year.

In this same time, too, the population in the city proper is expected to grow slowly from today's 7.2 million to 7.5 million by the end of the century. That will still be less than the 7.9 million it had in 1970, but it will reverse the more recent trend of population loss and represent a period of solid growth.

All in all, the general feeling is that New York's economic recovery will continue, and perhaps pick up steam. But even the city's most ardent champions warn that the extent to which it enters the new century in better shape than it is today will, in the long run, be determined by the visible progress made in dealing with its painful problems of poverty and race. That will be the acid test.

. . . and New York's tommorow

". . . I want to help bring people together. . . . I worry most about the division between rich and poor . . . that is the biggest problem of all. . . ."

". . . A spirit of renewal and optimism has taken root in New York. . . . And realism about the difficult choices [we must make] to keep our city solvent financially while compassionate and fair to all our citizens. . . . My own view of New York's future is a very optimistic one . . . a great international center, a true world city in commerce, in culture, in communication—and also in terms of its population . . . a future in which New York, and all the great cities of the world, will continue to represent the best of civilization, and remain the place for so many of the hopes and dreams of mankind."

—Mayor Edward I. Koch

AFTERWORD

By Dr. Nafis Sadik

In its short existence, the human race has already had a greater impact on its natural environment than all other species put together. We have produced more changes on the surface and the atmosphere of the planet than all the fires, floods, and natural upheavals in history. The greatest changes have come in the last few hundred years—and the engines of change have been the cities.

We usually think of change as progress. Certainly the possibilities of life have improved dramatically since 1800 in variety, quality, and availability. Even for the poorest, life is longer and opportunities for improving it more varied.

We assume that cities are the source of many of these good things. We look to the cities for cultural advance and intellectual innovation, sophistication in technology, and political and economic leadership.

There have always been critics of the price that cities demand. William Cobbett looked at eighteenth-century London with its toll of the young and the hopeful, its ruthless destruction of the poor and the inadequate, and called it "the Great Wen." But Dr. Johnson said that a man who was tired of London was tired of life. His central assumption—that cities are on balance a force for civilization and development—has never been seriously challenged since the industrial revolution saw the birth of the modern city.

But as the balance of world population shifts finally toward the city, it is time for a second look at our urban future. We are discovering the price that modern urbanization exacts. In the future, it may not be counted in the lives of individuals, but in the lives of nations. Instead of producers, the cities may have become parasites. The engines of change may have become the engines of destruction.

The pace and nature of population growth is itself a good reason for a second look at urbanization. With world population over five billion and racing toward six, eight, and perhaps ten billion a century from now, there are ominous warning signs that the natural environment may be reaching the limits of what it can absorb in the way of human interference. We may be in danger of destroying the ecosystem on which all our lives depend.

Much of the damage—acidification, a rising level of carbon dioxide in the atmosphere, too much ozone near the cities and too little in the stratosphere, the buildup of toxic wastes—is the result of industrial production and emissions. Most of it comes from industrialized countries with largely urban populations.

In developing countries, the major environmental problems are in rural areas—loss of groundwater, desertification, despoliation of the great watersheds and the tropical forests. Much of the damage is the result of the combined pressures of poverty and population growth.

This would be serious enough. But in their attempts to escape from the poverty-population trap, developing countries could be heading straight for another. In the past the answer to poverty and population growth was urbanization and industrial development. This book asks whether it is safe for developing countries to follow the same path: all the evidence says that it is not.

In the first place, population growth is much faster than it ever was in European countries, the United States, or Japan. It already threatens to overwhelm the cities of the developing world.

For another, the effort could be suicidal. Eight or ten billion people consuming resources and creating waste and pollution on the scale now common in the industrialized countries could simply overload the capacity of Earth to absorb them. Prosperity could then poison us.

New directions are needed. One will be to look afresh at the role of the city and what it offers. The search for a sustainable prosperity calls for new and safer technologies. They in turn may call for less concentration and more diffusion of populations. In an era of high-speed communication, the smaller city may come into its own as a place to live and work.

Another will undoubtedly be a direct attack on rapid population growth rates in developing countries, to ease pressure on resources, to slow urban growth and allow some time to develop policies of sustainable development. It may not be easy, but it is the only way, if we are to pass on to our children a world that is both urban and viable, that can sustain great numbers of people in peace and prosperity, and in harmony with the environment that supports them.

SELECTED REFERENCES

The following is not intended as a definitive bibliography on the subject. It merely indicates some of the references used in the preparation of this book. As noted in the Introduction, we also drew on reports and studies prepared in connection with the United Nations Population Fund's two conferences on Population and the Urban Future, and these are not listed individually.

Book of World City Rankings, by John T. Marlin, Immanuel Ness, and Stephen T. Collins, The Free Press, 1976

The Economist, July 5, 1986

The Expanding Metropolis, Seminar 9, Architectural Transformations in the Islamic World, The Aga Khan Award for Architecture, 1984

The Exploding Cities, by Peter Wilsher and Rosemary Richter, Quadrangle/The New York Times Book Co., 1975

"The Exploding Metropolis," Jim Antonio, *Arts, The Islamic World* (Vol. 2, no. 4), Winter 1984/85

The Future of Urbanization, by Jodi Jacobson and Lester R. Brown, Worldwatch Institute, 1987

Gaining People, Losing Ground, by Werner Fornos, the Population Institute and Science Press, 1988

Global Report on Human Settlements, United Nations Center for Human Settlements, 1986

The Home of Man, by Barbara Ward, W. W. Norton & Company, 1976

The New Landscape, by Charles Correa, The Book Society of India, 1985

Population and the Urban Future, United Nations Population Fund, 1980

Population and the Urban Future, United Nations Population Fund, 1986

Population Growth and Policies in Mega-Cities (Population Policy Papers), Population Division, United Nations, 1986

Population Images, United Nations Population Fund, 1987

"The Population Problem: Time Bomb or Myth?" by Robert S. McNamara, *Foreign Affairs,* Summer 1984

The Problems and Future of Bombay, by Rashmi Mayur, Urban Development Institute, Bombay, 1985

Prospects of World Urbanization, Population Division, United Nations, 1987

State of the World Population 1986, by Rafael M. Salas, United Nations Population Fund, 1986

State of the World Population 1988, by Nafis Sadik, United Nations Population Fund, 1988

State of the World, 1987, by Lester R. Brown and others, W. W. Norton, 1987

Summit Conference, Major Cities of the World, Tokyo Metropolitan Government, 1985

Toward the 21st Century, by Werner Fornos, the Population Institute, 1988

World Access to Birth Control, Population Crisis Committee, 1987

World Population Profile, United States Bureau of the Census, 1985

"The World's Urban Explosion," by Robert W. Fox, *National Geographic,* August 1984

INDEX